IT LEA~~~~ ~~~
THE SAME

A farmer's son in The Great War

IT LEAVES ME THE SAME

A farmer's son in The Great War

E.A. GREEN

Published under licence by Silver Crow Books and
The Self-Publishing Partnership, 7 Green Park Station, Bath BA1 1JB

www.silvercrowbooks.co.uk
www.selfpublishingpartnership.co.uk

ISBN printed book: 978-1-78545-324-3
ISBN e-book: 978-1-78545-325-0

Cover design by Kevin Rylands
Internal design by Andrew Easton

Printed and bound by CPI Group (UK) Ltd, Croydon, CR0 4YY

Ed Green was born in Shepton Mallet, Somerset in 1973 and this is his first book. He is the sixth generation to farm at Banks Farm, Chesterblade and he now lives with his two daughters in Frome, Somerset.

For
Allen John Green

CONTENTS

ACKNOWLEDGEMENTS

I would like to thank a number of individuals and organisations who have helped me research and write this book:

My cousin, Helen Turner, for having the foresight to investigate and save the Dorothy Bag, David and Gill Lindsay, for all their efforts to research and preserve the legacy of Allen's story, for their help and encouragement to write this book and for the use of some of their photos and documents, Jon Gliddon and Dav Baulch, for their time and effort to remember those in the Dorsetshire Regiment, for their research and for their encouragement, The Keep Military Museum in Dorchester, for taking on the role of custodians of Allen's artefacts, Frome Writers' Collective and Silver Crow Books, for all their help and support, especially Gill Harry and Brenda Bannister, John Payne, for editing and general encouragement, Alan Campbell, for sterling work editing the images, Charlotte de Grey and Douglas Walker at SPP, for all their help publishing this book, and all my family and friends, for all their continuous encouragement and support to me throughout.

PRELUDE

The Mormal Forest, France

D'autres bruits de combats ont troublé mon silence,
Et des troupes en marche ont foulé mes gazons
En des âges de haine et d'àpre violence,
Ou la guerre hurlait parmi mes frondaisons.

Sounds of combat disturb my silence,
And marching troops trample my lawns
And in times of hatred and violence,
War screams amongst my foliage.

PART ONE
OLD PHOTOS

1. A Photo on the Wall

A Green family portrait in 1918

He had always been watching over us all from the sepia photograph on the wall. My great uncle, Allen, dressed smartly in a rustic suit and tie, eighteen years of age and about to go to war. The year was 1918. In the picture, his right hand rests on his mother's shoulder in front of him. She is wearing a white blouse and long dark skirt, with a black choker around the neck. Small, circular glasses rest on her nose and her brown hair is tied up neatly. Allen's younger sister stands across from him, dressed in a white blouse and long skirt, her left hand resting on her father's shoulder creating symmetry with her older brother. The father sits straight and tall in a black suit jacket, waistcoat and tie, with brown trousers and boots. His has thin, neatly-combed hair and a large moustache. Between the two siblings at the back stands a severe looking older woman known as Aunt Pollie. She wears a black dress and her eyes stare at you, dark and intense. Thin, tight lips are held in a disapproving pose and she looks like she would have been a terror. At the front, between the two parents sits the youngest sibling, my grandfather, Jim, aged eleven and dressed in boots, long socks, tweed shorts and matching tweed suit jacket with waistcoat and tie.

But this story isn't about my grandfather; that's another whole book in itself. This story is about the life of my great uncle, Allen John Green, and the time he grew up in.

2. A Bag in the Attic

I remember the phone call in 2011. After answering it, my mother called out.

'Your cousin, Helen, found a bag of old stuff when she and Dave were sorting out the attic. I think you're going to be interested in what they've found. When did you want to move those cattle 'cause I want to get on and do some things in the garden?'

It had been around ten years since I'd had a cursory look into our family tree. Now, in a Somerset farmhouse at Easton Hill Farm in East Pennard, a few miles down the road from our home in Chesterblade, Helen (a great niece of Allen's sister, Elsie) had found an old musty-looking bag which would lead me to a new involvement with the past. The attic was in the farmhouse where Elsie had lived. Helen's brother, Dave, now lived there. He had sadly lost his wife a few years earlier while their two children were still young and Helen was helping him clear out the attic of the old family home. The bag had been very close to being thrown out, as the attic had been full with a vast array of old items gathering dust. Luckily, my cousin recognised that this particular bag might be something special. Hence her phone call to my mum.

3. THE KITCHEN - 2011

Various members of my family gathered in my parents' kitchen to see the old bag that had been found. My parents were there, and my two sisters. Helen put the bag on the kitchen table. It was an old cloth bag, issued to soldiers in the Great War to keep their personal belongings in, and which had become known as a 'Dorothy Bag'.

Allen's Dorothy Bag and contents

Upon hearing from nurses how difficult it was to safeguard the personal belongings of sick and wounded soldiers admitted to the hospitals and Casualty Clearing Stations near battlefields, Lady Smith Dorrien decided to do something to help. In April 1915, she contacted her husband who was a General commanding the 2nd Army in France, and asked if a small bag would help solve the problem. He replied that he needed fifty thousand as soon as possible, so she set about establishing an appeal fund to buy material and a depot from where they could be distributed. For the first year, Lady Smith Dorrien's house in London was used as the collection depot, after which the operation moved twice, to addresses of acquaintances in London. The Queen Mary Needlework Guild helped organise supplies of materials from workers worldwide.

Donations paid for the material while volunteers gave their time to make the bags. Initially they were made from plain unbleached calico material but changed to the use of brighter colours after requests from the men. We didn't realise it at the time, but Allen's bag was a very rare example of an original 'Dorothy Bag', with the only other example anyone knows of being in the Imperial War Museum in London. Around two million were made and sent to soldiers during the war. Allen's bag, measuring around twelve inches by fourteen, had a green flowered criss-cross pattern set against a light background with dots on. A double pull-string gathered in the neck to prevent anything falling out. A label, two inches from the bottom, long since faded, provided a space for the soldier's name and rank. Upon soldiers being admitted to hospital, the bags would be hung on the patients' bedposts. Helen carefully pulled out a mud-encrusted leather tobacco pouch and a pipe. The wooden pipe had a beautifully made walnut end with the words 'Captain Comfy' and 'MADE IN FRANCE' embossed on its sides, so it must have been purchased by Allen while in France. Unbelievably, the tobacco pouch still has some tobacco left inside. Soldiers in the war had a rum and tobacco ration, although this was at the volition of the commanding officer to allow or deny. Rations were kept at a Service Reserve Depot or SRD which became translated by soldiers as Seldom Reaches Destination as commanding officers were known for keeping the rations for themselves. There was also an old red leather wallet, which was empty inside, and a set of four silk regimental badges which turned out to be made by John Player and Sons in 1916 and would have been inside his army tobacco or cigarette rations.

Allen's cigarette silks

Lastly, there was an old tin. Helen opened it and drew out the old bits of paper from inside. The first piece of paper was carefully unfolded and turned out to be an army medical examination card dated 16 May 1917. There was an upside down oval rubber stamp that read, 'RECRUITING MEDICAL BOARD TAUNTON'.

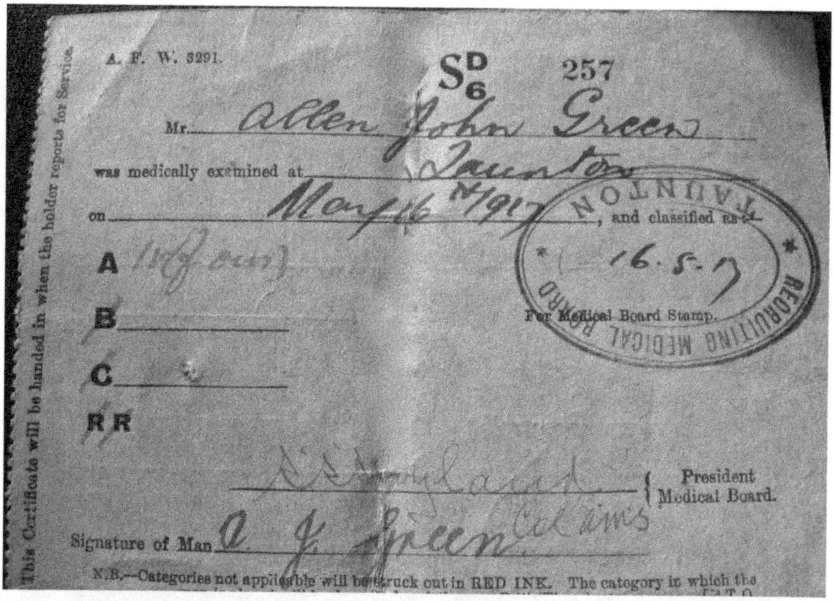

A. F. W. 3291.

S^D_6 257

Mr. Allen John Green

was medically examined at Taunton

on May 16th 1917, and classified as

A 1 (If occur)

B

C

RR

TAUNTON * 16.5.17 * RECRUITING MEDICAL BOARD

For Medical Board Stamp.

President Medical Board.

Signature of Man A. J. Green

N.B.—Categories not applicable will be struck out in RED INK. The category in which the

This Certificate will be handed in when the holder reports for Service.

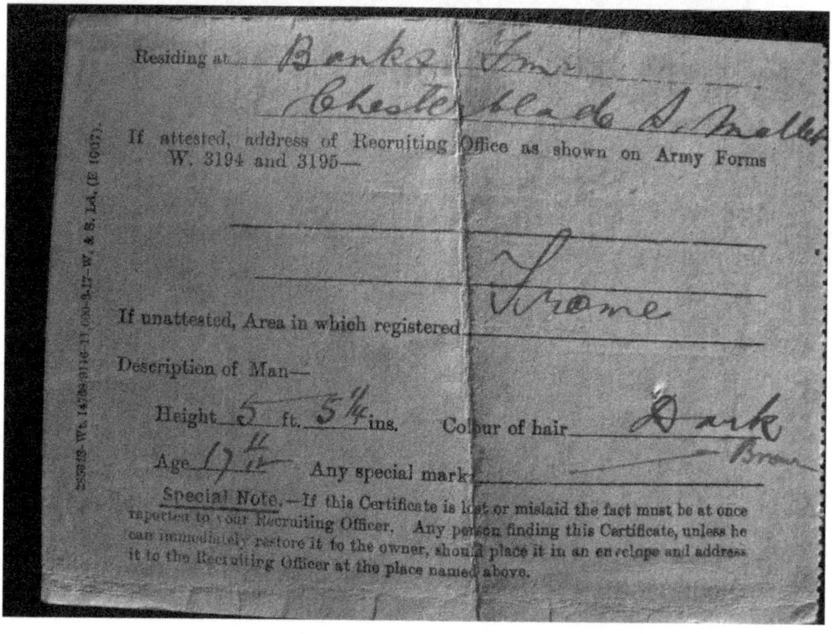

Residing at Banks Fm

Chesterblade S. Mallet

If attested, address of Recruiting Office as shown on Army Forms W. 3194 and 3195—

If unattested, Area in which registered Frome

Description of Man—

Height 5 ft. 5¼ ins. Colour of hair Dark

Age 17 11/12 Any special mark — Brown

Special Note.—If this Certificate is lost or mislaid the fact must be at once reported to your Recruiting Officer. Any person finding this Certificate, unless he can immediately restore it to the owner, should place it in an envelope and address it to the Recruiting Officer at the place named above.

Allen's Army Certificate of Exemption

The card was signed by Allen. Someone else had filled in his residence as *'Banks Farm, Chesterblade'* and the area he was registered to as *'Frome'*. His height was recorded as five feet, five and a quarter inches, his hair as dark brown and his age as 17 $^{11}/_{12}$ years old, so almost at the point of conscription age.

Allen's July 1917 Tribunal Certificate

When war broke out in August 1914, the British Government asked for one hundred thousand volunteers to join the army. However, there was a stampede of volunteer recruits that far exceeded expectations and resources were stretched to cope with the numbers. By the end of September 1914, seven hundred and fifty thousand volunteers had signed up and then on average another one hundred and twenty-five thousand per month enrolled. It is estimated that around two hundred and fifty thousand British boys lied about their age in order to join up. The youngest was found to be just twelve and was duly sent home.

A National Registration Act in 1915 drew up and targeted a list of men eligible to fight, although in May of that year the War Office was instructed not to accept 'skilled workers' from farms that were needed to feed the nation. By the autumn, the Derby scheme was introduced whereby 'starred' labourers exempt from military duty had to attest their willingness to serve. This was set against a backdrop of the stigmatisation of any hint of cowardice, especially when so many families were losing loved ones in battle. A feature of the times involved older ladies handing white feathers to so-called 'fit' men who hadn't gone off to fight. By 1916, however, the government introduced the Military Service Act calling up single men between the ages of eighteen and forty-one, and agricultural workers now had to apply for exemptions.

My cousin, Helen, then pulled out a collection of old pieces of paper from Allen's cloth bag. On the first piece, a Tribunal Notice dated 10 July 1917 relating to Allen states, 'The man be exempted from being called up for military service'.

A second piece of paper reads:

ARMY RESERVE B

VOLUNTARY ATTESTED MAN

CERTIFICATE OF EXEMPTION

The old orange coloured document is dated 13 July 1917 and lists the council offices in Shepton Mallet as the local tribunal and states Allen as '*18 years old*' in the Frome area whose occupation is '*Assisting in Managing Farm*'. The exemption is '*Conditional till substitute is found*'.

Allen's July 1917 Tribunal Decision document

The family therefore now needed to find more help on the farm if Allen was to leave and join the army. An advertisement was placed in the local newspaper the *Western Gazette* in April 1918. It read '*HELP (good) WANTED, farm-house. Opportunity to learn cheese-making. Apparatus used. Three in family, youngest ten. – Mrs. GREEN, Banks Farm, Chesterblade, Shepton Mallet.*'

It's hard to imagine now how living through these times must have been and how the family would have been feeling. In July 1917, the war had been going on for nearly three years. Allen had reached conscription age and his exemption from the war was only until someone else could be found to take his place on the farm to undertake the work. The sense of trepidation must have been enormous.

The German spring offensives in 1918 saw the repeal of the protection measures for full-time agricultural labourers which had been introduced in 1916. After the Bolshevik uprising in Russia, Germany was now able to pull troops and resources away from the Eastern front and push harder on the Western front. The consequence for Britain was that more troops were now needed to combat this renewed offensive.

My cousin laid out more faded paper from Allen's bag on the kitchen table. The first piece was a letter, addressed to Allen from the Somerset Agricultural Executive Committee, and related to another tribunal hearing the following spring in 1918 that would decide if Allen was to be sent to war:

A hundred years after the family received these papers, our eyes eagerly followed the words down two faded notices sent following the Military Service Act of 1918, to understand how Allen's fate had unfolded. The next old document declared that Allen was able to appeal his conscription into the army and his appeal would be heard in Bath on 4 June 1918:

Somerset Agricultural Executive Committee.

Secretary:
NORMAN OLDFIELD,
68, BOULEVARD, WESTON-SUPER-MARE.
Tel. 373.

AGRICULTURE AND RECRUITING.

WITHDRAWAL OF EXEMPTIONS OF MEN BORN IN THE
YEARS 1895, 1896, 1897, 1898 AND 1899.

DEAR SIR,

I am in receipt of your communication and enclose

(1) Form of particulars (F.P.250/L.I.) required by the Executive Committee.

(2) Form of application to the Appeal Tribunal (in duplicate).

Please complete these forms with the greatest care, and return them to me *without delay*, when I will lay the case before the Executive Committee.

In the event of the Executive Committee being satisfied that the man in question is a highly skilled agricultural worker, whole time employed on a farm in farm work, and that he is irreplaceable and essential to the cultivation of the farm, the application (in duplicate) will be handed to the Somerset Appeal Tribunal and you will in due course receive a notification of the date and place of hearing.

Yours faithfully,
NORMAN OLDFIELD,
Secretary.

Mr. S. Green,
Banks Farm.
Chesterblade

With reference to an application to the Appeal Tribunal which is being lodged by your employer, - will you please hand the enclosed papers to him to deal with and return to me.

F. B. ESMONDE-WHITE.

To :-
Mr. A. J. Green
Chesterblade
Shepton Mallet.

National Service Representative,
Room No. 8. Shire Hall,
Taunton.

16 MAY 1918

A letter to Allen in May 1918 from the Somerset Agricultural Executive Committee

R. 66. *Appeal Tribunal for* SOMERSET (Bath).

Appellant or other party
(Not National Service Rep.).

Address Sidney House,
Boulevard,
WESTON-SUPER-MARE.

Date 30 MAY 1918

NOTICE OF HEARING.

Notice is hereby given that the ~~appeal against the decision of the~~

application ~~Local Tribunal~~ in respect

of ALLEN JOHN GREEN

will be heard at the Guildhall, Bath,

on Tuesday

the 4th day of June , 1918, at or about

2 o'clock in the after- noon.

(30180) W7351/86 10,000 5/18 A. P. & S. Ld.

Allen's Notice for his appeal in Bath on 4 June 1918

So Allen was to attend a tribunal to see if he would be going to war or not. What a job for a committee of people to have to do. What a huge decision they would have to make about someone's life: to make a decision about whether or not to send an eighteen-year-old farm boy to the front.

There were no further documents relating to the tribunal or its decision. The next document to come out of the bag was a letter, written in ink, in Allen's handwriting. It was dated sixteen days after the tribunal hearing:

20.6.1918 Taunton

Dear Mother,

I am getting on alright up to now, so don't worry. As soon as I got to the barracks I had to make up my bed, consists 3 boards, bag of straw and 3 or 4 blankets and a hard pillow. I can tell you I was damn tired after sticking about all day. There are about 24 in our room. Some of them could not go to sleep because their bed was so hard but I could. We had to get up at 5.30 wash and parade at 7. Breakfast at 8 o'clock consists of packet 2 pieces of bread and a great dish of tea. Well Mother if we get such good living as we get today I shan't grumble. They had us out about 11 o'clock and told us what we had to join up in. They have put me in the 3rd Dorsets and all those over 19 and we are oft to Weymouth tomorrow Friday, I'm glad. I should not like to stop in Taunton very long. Those under 19 are oft to Ireland. I'm glad I'm not going there, just out of it. I got my full kit, can you imagine me in Khaki. I have sent on my togs tonight. I don't know if it will be sent to Shepton. If Dad calls round tomorrow it might be there. It is no use to write before you here (sic) from me again. Well Mother give my love to dear old Jim, Dad, Elsie and all the rest of the Chesterblade people, and tell them not to worry.

  With love
  From Allen
  P.S. How is the haymaking getting on.

So the tribunal had rejected Allen's application to keep running the family farm and grow food for the nation; it was deemed better to send him to war. What a contrast he must have found leaving the countryside and shacking up in crowded barracks with a multitude of others.

The *Shepton Mallet Journal* reported the tribunal hearing result in its pages on 7th June 1918. It reads:

Allen John Green, 18, of Banks Farm, Chesterblade, was appealed for by his father, Sidney Green. He was a very hard working youth, skilled at all kinds of farm work, and was helping to increase the food supply. He did the ploughing and sowing and was going to do the reaping.

The Chairman: You are much better suited than nine tenths of the farmers with regards to labour. You are on velvet compared to some of them. The Government has asked for these men. The industrial world has been stripped to the bone of labour. Some of the thousands of young men on the farms must now go. – Application refused.

Another dusty letter dated two days after the first was then put on the kitchen table in front of us all. It is in Allen's handwriting again and addressed to my grandfather who would have been eleven years old:

22.6.1918 Weymouth

Dear Jim,

I hope Mother received my letter I wrote Thursday. We are at Wyke Regis Camp now, there are about 1,000 strong now, all in the Dorsets. I'm sleeping in a tent, there are 11 of us in it, we have got a bed and blankets and are as thick as bees in a hive. I have a good mate his name is Cary from Frome, nearly all are farmer's sons, a decent lot. Some of them in other tents are so noisy as hell (old soldiers). We have just had our numbers so I can write. I should like a little bit of cheese sent on about a pound. We do not get anything from 4pm to 8am.

Four or five of us are going to Weymouth this afternoon, we are about 2 mile from Weymouth, not very far from Portland by train. You have received my parcels I hope. I shall like it when I get used to it, it is rather funny to begin. So don't worry, give them all love

from Allen

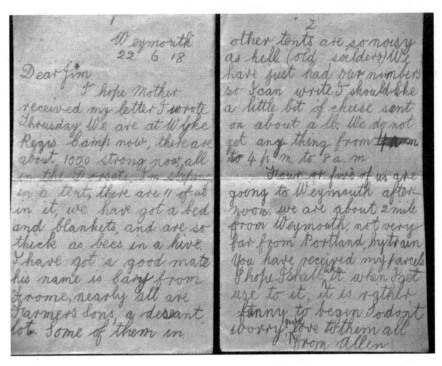

Allen's letter to his brother 22 June 1918

After the disastrous Gallipoli campaign, wounded Anzac soldiers from Australia and New Zealand began to arrive in Weymouth in June 1915 to convalesce in the nearby village of Chickerell. Locals organised a strawberry and cream tea welcome event and the wounded soldiers began attending church services and socialising with local families on Sundays. Local women soon began to be charmed by the men from down under and fifty weddings took place. Some Anzacs would never return home again and eighty-six are buried in local cemeteries. During the course of the war over one hundred and five thousand Anzacs would arrive in the area to recuperate and this connection has led to Weymouth observing Anzac Day on 25th April every year since the war with a service along the esplanade at the Anzac Memorial.

4. A FAMILY PORTRAIT

When I think back to this moment in 2011 and the time my cousin brought over the extraordinary bag of artefacts and memories from a hundred years ago, I remember how incredible it was to hold in my hand things that were so old and yet so present. After he had been just a face in an old photograph for so many years, Allen's story came to life. The more I discovered about him, the more intrigued I became with his story and wondered what it would have been like to live in his world.

Allen in 1918 and the same chair today in the same position in front of the house we both grew up in

When I was growing up as a child, I never really took any notice of the photo or the people staring out from its age old frame. They were just relics from a time long past; ancestors that were my flesh and blood yet too distant to mean much to me, standing in front of flowerbeds at my family home.

The year it was taken was extraordinary. The war that was meant to have been over by Christmas, in 1914, was still continuing nearly four years later and thousands had died in a brutal mass conflict the like of which the world had never seen. German submarine attacks were cutting off Britain's food supplies and farms were struggling to produce enough food to feed the nation. The government was running out of men to fight, which was probably why Allen was called up for military service as soon as he turned eighteen.

As well as the family photograph on the wall, and the letter to Jim, my grandfather, when he was a young boy at boarding school in the nearby town of Shepton Mallet, my parents had two other sepia photographs in their possession. One photograph must have been taken at the same time as the family portrait that hung on the wall. Allen was dressed in the same clothes as in the previous photograph, and sitting on the same chair that his father, Sidney, was sitting on, in the framed picture on the wall. Additionally, the photograph was taken in the same spot in front of the house I was to grow up in.

In it, Allen is shown sitting up straight on the chair, his hands clasped neatly and resting in front of him. The country suit and tie and white shirt match the neatness of his brown hair and his face bears a serious expression. He is about to go to war, and this photograph, together with the family portrait taken at the same time, must have been taken specially, as a record. After three and a half years of fighting, so many had already been killed and so many sons and brothers had not come home again that this photo session before going away must have been incredibly emotional for them all. No-one in the picture is smiling. The wooden handmade chair sits to this day in my parents' front hallway. When I walk by it, it is as if Allen's spirit still holds there somehow and watches over us as we go about our daily lives.

The second of the two photographs is of Allen in the khaki uniform of the Dorsetshire Regiment which he described in his first letter home after conscription. This photograph had been printed on a postcard and cropped into an oval shape; it shows Allen from the lower chest up, in khaki army uniform jacket and matching hat. The material looks thick, uncomfortable and itchy and is adorned with brass buttons and a regiment badge on the hat. His facial expression is calm and less serious than in the family portraits taken at home. This portrait was taken shortly after conscription and before leaving for France.

Allen newly conscripted in khaki uniform in 1918

PART TWO
BEFORE THE WAR

1. Life Before The Great War

My family were Somerset farmers before the Great War, and I'm now the sixth generation to farm the same piece of land.

Allen's story first came to my attention when I was still at school. I was studying English as one of my A-levels at Sexey's School in the nearby town of Bruton and the poets of the First World War were on the syllabus that year. Little did I know then how their work and experiences would come back into my life. Nor did I realise how much this period had shaped my own future. My generation have enjoyed peace and it is hard to imagine what it would have been like to be at war. Even though I was a teenager who didn't really know anything of the world, the words of poets such as Owen and Sassoon were powerful and affecting.

I remember coming home from school and mentioning the war poets we were studying. My parents took down the photo that had hung on the wall unnoticed and pointed out Allen.

'That's your great uncle. He fought in the First World War. Your father's named after him and your middle name comes from him too.'

I had always presumed my middle name had been a hand-me-down from my father; a throwback to an old fashioned, more patriarchal time, when parents gave their children their own Christian name in the hope this would somehow make them the same as them. I thought this practice pretty unimaginative when there are so many names to choose from. I had hated my name; Edward Allen Green. I never came across anyone else with these names at school and thought they sounded antiquated and square. At the time, there was a cool kid in my class at school whose name was Stephen, so in an attempt to put this right, I made demands aged ten to change my name to Stephen by deed poll. My hope was that adopting my class mate's name would transfer some of his golden aura to me. My parents didn't agree.

I didn't think much more about my great uncle until about ten years later when I developed a mild interest in tracing the family tree. When I came to the branch which included Allen, I found out more about his war experiences in France but there was very little to go on at this point. My grandfather, Allen's younger brother, had died a few years earlier, so there wasn't anyone around anymore to flesh out his story and I was left to piece together what I could.

Allen was born in 1899 in Charfield, Gloucestershire, the first child of Sidney and Mabel Green, who had married that same year. Sidney Green, 31 years old at the time, was a livestock farmer at Millhouse Farm in the small hamlet of Chesterblade in Somerset, which nestles on the edge of the Mendip Hills. He had four brothers and four sisters. Mabel, 26 years old when they married, hailed from the Osborne family, and they farmed at Banks Farm at the other end of Chesterblade. This was not that unusual in those days, as most countryside dwellers did not travel far and a 'good marriage' would also consolidate some farming aspirations. According to my father, the Osborne family were 'of much greater repute' and the Greens were 'a bit of a scruffy lot', so their marriage would have made for interesting local gossip.

Upon their marriage, Sidney and Mabel moved from Chesterblade and started farming at Peking Mill, near Evercreech, two miles away. Two more siblings were born: Elsie in 1902 and my grandfather, Jim, in 1907. The farm was located near Evercreech Junction railway station where a regular livestock market was held, with the emphasis on calves. Buyers would transport their livestock via train or along the roads if they lived more locally. Sidney also purchased corn from the station to take back home to grind up and sell on to other farmers for pig fattening. Today at Peking Mill, there remains a shabby looking pub that never seems to be doing very well.

An anecdote from that time relates how one day Sidney was following the stream from Peking Mill to the family farm at Mill House in Chesterblade and had stopped to 'tickle trout' at a place known as 'Up The Rocks' just above the village of Stoney Stratton. The Hill family, who farmed around that part of the stream, saw him catching fish and reported him to the police. Sidney was summonsed and subsequently fined.

In 1908, Sidney's father died at Mill House Farm and Sidney's brother, John, carried on running the farm there. John would later move to Rock Farm in Stoney Stratton. My father recalls how my grandfather, Jim, talked about visiting his grandparents at Mill House Farm and there would be steamed puddings in muslin cloth tied up to the wooden beam in the kitchen. Jim and Allen would go out rabbiting and come back hungry so would take down one of these puddings without their grandmother knowing and eat it. So that this would remain unnoticed, they would refill the muslin cloth with barley meal or sawdust and hang it back up on the wooden beam. If their grandmother started to reach up and get down one of the already eaten puddings at a meal time, the boys would scarper before they could get scolded.

Rabbiting was an important food source at this time. The *Shepton Mallet Journal* on 18 January 1918 reports *'On Monday the order fixing prices for rabbits came into operation, 2/- with fur or 1/9 skinned. The killing of rabbits is deemed by the Government as a national and public service due to crop protection and food supply. Every rabbit killed represents 2lb of food for the nation and one enemy less for crops and the farmer'.*

We still have at home a collection of old papers, farm sale brochures and documents, with some dating right back as far as the 1700s. Among these old papers is a letter to Sidney from the family solicitor Dyne, Muller & Hughes in Bruton dated 1909 that contains his father's will. The will had been updated in 1907 when one of Sidney's brothers, Frederick, had died at the age of 47, although no-one today knows why. The executors and beneficiaries of Frederick's will are named as Sidney, John and Mary. Mary was a spinster and became known as Aunt Pollie and was to live with Sidney's family in later years. Three other siblings had also died prematurely. Emily, had died back in 1868 aged only two years old, Samuel had died in 1882 aged nineteen, and William had died in 1904 aged forty nine. So, by 1907, four out of Sidney's eight siblings had already died.

I have a notebook dated 1908 written in Sidney's hand which details the farm sale at Mill House Farm following the death of his father. The sale was undertaken by the auctioneers Wainwright, Laver & Crees Ltd from Shepton Mallet.

The handwritten notebook details meticulously line by line the lot numbers, description and price to be paid for all the sale lots. As well as the sale of the old fashioned farm implements relating to hand milking cows, cheese making and cider making, there is also a list of various batches of pigs and cattle sold. The cattle are listed by their names, such as *'Whiteface'*, *'Lily'* and *'Cockup'*, a wistful practice, common then, but less so now.

A notebook written in Sidney's hand dated 1912 lists on each page farming customers who were purchasers of animal feed from him. Each purchase is dated with the price paid and a description of the feed which includes things like *barley, dairy cake, oats, bran, maize* and *poultry meal.*

In 1913, aged fourteen, Allen and his family moved from Peking Mill back to their home village of Chesterblade to his mother's family's home farm at Banks Farm, the house in front of which the family photo in 1918 was taken. In preparation for Sidney and Mabel to take over the farm, the Osbornes sold their one hundred and fifteen Shorthorn milking cows to make room for the milking cows the Greens would be bringing with them.

Banks Farmhouse mid 20th century

The dairy cattle listed in the catalogue all have their names listed next to the lot number, such as '*Tulip*', '*Buttercup*' and '*Brandy*'. Shorthorn cattle today have lost favour to more commercial Holstein and Friesian breeds, although small numbers do still exist.

The list of implements gives a great indication of how the farm was running in 1913 just prior to the outbreak of the war when Allen was fourteen years old. Tractors had not yet been introduced and all the work was done by horse power and manual labour. Cars were not widely in use yet either, with horse and trap as the main mode of transport. The section in the catalogue regarding conveyances from the various railway stations to the sale illustrates the importance of the railway at that time too. The Shepton Mallet railway station has long since closed down and the town is no longer serviced by railway tracks. The Cranmore station still exists as the East Somerset Steam Railway; it is now a tourist attraction and chuffs its passengers along a two mile stretch of railway track.

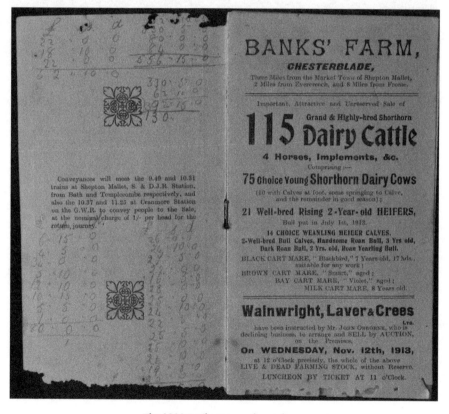

The 1913 Banks Farm sale catalogue

We still have three purchasing slips written in Sidney's hand that list all his purchases at his father-in-law's sale that day and the prices paid next to the lot numbers. There is also an old red notebook written in Allen's hand which contains a list of all the sale lots with the prices paid next to them with a grand total for the sale of £2541 12s. 0d.

Allen's notebook from the 1913 Banks Farm sale

We still have a 1913 newspaper cutting about the sale from the local newspaper, the *Shepton Mallet Journal*. It reads:

DISPERSAL OF A WELL-KNOWN HERD

On Wednesday in last week the herd of Mr. John Osborne, of Chesterblade, who has been in business for 43 years, and is now retiring, was disposed of by

Messrs. Wainwright, Laver & Crees, the well-known firm of auctioneers, of Shepton Mallet. The sale was conducted by Mr. S. H. Cross, who, in opening the proceedings, expressed his regret and that of the firm at the retirement of Mr. Osborne, who had been such a first-class agriculturist, and had done so much to advance the interests of agriculture in the county. There was a very large attendance, agriculturists being present from Nottingham, Wolverhampton, Worcester, Gloucester, Hampshire, South Wales, Hereford, Dorset, and many from this district. Before the sale commenced, about 700 sat down to a luncheon supplied by Mr. J. S. Williams, of Shepton Mallet, and served in a large marquee. The chair was taken by Mr. John Whitehead, of Lydford, who was supported by Mr. Jn. Cary and Mr. R. J. Hoskins and others.

The sale commenced with the implements, high prices being realised. Next came the dispersal of the herd of 115 cattle, which sold readily at exceptional prices. A fine cow and calf were sold to Mr. Allesbrook for £38 10s, and the same gentleman also bought two other lots for £28 10s and £26 respectively ... Mr. A. Allen, of Chesterblade, secured some fine animals at £20 and £23 10s (twice) ... Mr. S. Green, the incoming tenant, bought 16 at an average price of £24 5s ... The dairy cows made an average of nearly £24 each, whilst the two-year-old heifers ranged from £31 to £37 per pair. The yearlings made from £8 to £10 10s each. Five small heifer calves weaned in June made £43, a fine two-year-old bull was sold for £27, a smart young bull fetched £22 5s, and a nice young roan bull calf £21. Another changed owners at £13. Mr. Green purchased a very smart black mare for 50 guineas. The other lots sold at good prices. Considering that it was not a full pedigree herd the prices must be considered exceptionally good. The sale as a whole was considered to have been one of the most successful ever held in the county of Somerset.

On the back of the newspaper cutting, some advertisements are very much of their time:

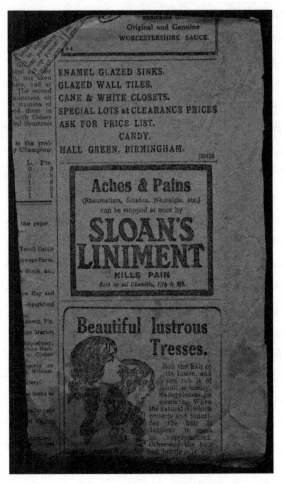

1913 Shepton Mallet Journal advertisements

My father recalls my grandfather talking about how when he was a lad Grandfather Osborne would go off to Shepton Mallet livestock market in a horse and cart and would come home sozzled with booze at the end of the day. The old horse would know the way home so he would nod off to sleep by the time they reached home. However, if the gate was shut into the yard at home, the horse would turn around and head back to Shepton

Mallet whilst the still-inebriated farmer dozed blissfully unaware in the horse drawn cart.

Chesterblade at this time consisted of around seventeen cottages and houses; most, if not all, of them were inhabited by farmers and farm workers. Houses at that time had not accrued the value and stature of today's housing market. Farm work was carried out by a multitude of hands and all this labour and their families needed accommodation on the farm.

The value of the houses in Chesterblade today now outstrips the value of the land on which they were built, even though land has seen a spike in value in recent years. Various financial crises have led investors to sink money into land, as it's now seen as a safe asset that will retain its value at a time when interest rates have been at unprecedented lows. Farming is very different compared to Allen's day. Very little farm labour is now required to carry out the same farming tasks, due to efficiencies from mechanisation, so the houses in the village no longer need to accommodate those that work on the land. When a house is sold in Chesterblade, estate agent spiel talks of 'location, location, location', and prices reach over a million pounds at the upper end of the houses on offer.

Most of the traditional stone buildings that were cow stalls, pig pens or stores for feed and fodder back in 1913, have now been turned into tasteful barn conversions for human habitation, with the old farmhouse feel of stone floors and wood beams a desirable asset. Only last year, we converted a yard of old stone buildings that in Allen's day used to consist of cow stalls, a bull pen and a shed for hay carts, into a luxury four-bedroom holiday let with wifi and 'great views'. The countryside is now a recreational escape for urban dwellers, with food production of somewhat secondary importance, especially when food imports are so cheap and readily available. Footpaths, that once had a functional use linking settlements across fields, are now bridleways and leisure highways for dog walkers.

But some things have not changed much since 1913. Other than the houses, the other features of significance in Chesterblade are the post box (a rare Victorian era model inset into the wall) and St. Mary's Chapel, where most of my family on my father's side are buried. Although the churchyard was not in use as a burial ground prior to 1890, the chapel, nestled amongst yew trees, dates back eight hundred years to Norman times and has undergone many alterations in its lifetime.

In 1887, just prior to Allen's birth, major alterations were undertaken to commemorate the Golden Jubilee of the reign of Queen Victoria. In 1888, Allen's family is recorded as having given a new brass lectern and brass chandelier to the church. The church became licensed for weddings in 1901. The stained glass windows were commissioned from Howard Travers of London with the result exhibited at the Royal Academy in London in 1913 and installed later that year.

St. Mary's Chapel with our family graves in the foreground

One other significant feature of Chesterblade is the prominent hill that rises up to the south of the hamlet known as Smalldown Knoll. Excavations have indicated this pre-dates Roman times and was actually an Iron Age fort. It now lies covered in grass. Chesterblade's name originates from the ancient fort: 'Ceaster' in Latin refers to a fort and 'blade' to a ledge or terrace, or in this case, hill. In 1065 it was known as 'Chestreblad'. A Somerset Plea in A.D. 1225 records the name as 'Cestrebald', and finally 'Chesterblade' in 1327.

The hill fort covers around five acres and contains fourteen barrows (raised burial sites) within a double rampart outer perimeter. Exploratory excavations in 1904 by a Mr Gray found Bronze Age pottery. A ley line runs through here, and a now-unused trigonometry point, made of concrete and metal, marks the hill out as a high point at two hundred and twenty-two metres above sea level. The hill can be seen for miles around and provides spectacular three hundred and sixty degree views. Cranmore Tower, Alfred's Tower in Wiltshire, and Glastonbury Tor can all be viewed from here, and on a clear day, Hinkley Point power station on the North Somerset coast and Dorset to the south can be seen. You can feel a sense of history when standing on top of the hill and the old presence of the many that have trodden its turf through the ages.

Back down in the village, Joseph Allen, who used to farm at Manor Farm in the late 1800s before his son Arthur took over in 1905, found evidence of a Roman villa at Manor Farm. This included foundations, pot shards, a lamp and coins, some dating back to A.D. 270-400.

In 1790, the vicar, a Reverend Jenkyns, wrote *'Within memory the land at Chesterblade had been largely given over to tillage, but with the increase in the price of cheese had been converted to pasture or meadow much improved by the use of blue marl which is raised here'*. As dairy farming became predominant going into the nineteenth century, the small agricultural community in

1801 counted fourteen households eligible for payment of church and poor rates. In 1811 the total population was one hundred and twelve, consisting of fifty-four males and fifty-eight females.

A succinct description of how others find the village was illustrated well by Arthur Mee, the editor of *Somerset, County of Romantic Splendour* in 1940. He described his experience of Chesterblade thus:

'*It has a small church charming on its own little hill, and the stem of an old cross under an ancient yew 13 feet around the trunk. Dawn breaks on the village behind the steep Small Down, where Roman coins and pottery have been found; I have seen them in Taunton Museum.*

We left the haymakers just over the Churchyard wall and came into this lovely place through outer doors like a barn's and through an inner doorway which has welcomed twenty-five generations of village folk, for it was fashioned by the Normans.'

In his memoirs, Arthur Allen, who farmed at Manor Farm following his father's retirement, recalls boyhood memories of the church services in the late 1800s:

'*Practically everyone in the hamlet attended these divine services in those days, and the small church was comfortably filled. On the occasion of the Annual Harvest Festivals the church was always packed with people. It was adorned on those occasions with loving care by the mothers and their daughters of the few farmers and their workpeople living in the hamlet. Apart from every variety of fruit and flowers there were bunches of neatly arranged turnips, parsnips and carrots with potatoes, wheat, barley, oats and mangel-wurzel*'.

As with many things, whilst some things change, much remains the same, such as field names. To me those names are akin to the charm and heritage of the shipping forecast, each revealing a glimpse of the personality of that particular field. The fields back then that I still farm today had names such as Fuzzy Ground, Goblets, Goosehole, Winterwell, Poison Ground and Old Ruins. You might think that fields don't have a personality, but they do. Animals behave a certain way in different fields and the ambience changes dramatically between different areas of the farm. For example, cattle enjoy lying on the top part of a field known as Ladycroft, but are restless whenever they graze a field known as Broadway Hill. It is hard to fathom why this is.

In 1913, the family were farming around one hundred and seventy acres. A notebook from around this time, with Sidney's name on, lists in detail grass seed prescription rates as advised by the North of Scotland College. The farm was endeavouring to innovate with the times to get the most production from grassland, which is very much the zeitgeist again today. The dairy cows would calve in February and the calves be weaned off in April and herded down the four miles of road on foot to the calf sales at Evercreech Junction, close to where the family lived previously at Peking Mill. The cows would then milk off the spring and summer grass and cheese making would begin in earnest once the work of rearing the calves was finished. The whey from the cheese making would then be used to feed up pigs for fattening. Slabs of cotton cake came in from the colonies around the world and swedes and mango turnips were grown on the farm for animal feed. A small area of barley and wheat was also grown with the corn and ground up for additional feed. In the summer months, grass was cut and dried into hay for feeding in the winter months when the grass had stopped growing. Barley and wheat straw was used to make a waterproof thatch on top of the hayricks stacked in the fields for feeding the cows in the winter. Strips of hazel cut from the woodland copses down in the field called Goosehole would be bent into a U shape and used as spars to pin down and keep the thatch together on top of the hayricks. It was a holistic system that worked with the seasons beautifully.

The technological advances that we see today allow us to do things that we wouldn't otherwise do and this is in conflict with what nature and the natural flow of the seasons suggest we should do. In harmony with the seasons, the milking cows in 1913 would be dried off from milking as the harshest part of the winter approached before Christmas. This made complete sense for both the animals, who no longer had the best summer grass to eat, and also for the humans who would not have to milk over the Christmas period and during the coldest, wettest part of the year.

Milking at this time was done by hand and a worker with good technique would be able to milk around ten cows an hour, sat on a stool squeezing milk from the teats into a bucket. There would be a group of ten people working together on this on the farm in 1913. Today, one person in a mechanised milking parlour can milk around a hundred cows an hour on their own. Needless to say, this is done all year round with no break for anyone and through the coldest, wettest months of the year. Four o'clock starts are the norm as electricity means darkness is no longer much of a hindrance to producing milk. I wonder if we would have better lives if we went back to working in harmony with the seasons and daylight hours as we once had to. Technological advancement should improve our quality of life but often only enables more work.

As well as much more labour being required in 1913 compared to now, the other mainstay of farm work was the use of horses. At this time, the use of tractors was very much in its infancy with less than a thousand crankshaft-style machines in use across Britain, and this mostly in the main crop growing regions outside of the south west. This compares to the three hundred and ten thousand tractors officially registered today that are now spread throughout all agricultural sectors and have an unprecedented speed and efficiency. One person on a tractor today can plough one acre in fifteen minutes. In 1913, a farmer running a two-horse single furrow plough would take a whole day to plough the same area. At Banks Farm, the first tractors didn't arrive until the end of the Second World War so horses were at the forefront of farm work in 1913.

The way livestock are moved from place to place has also changed dramatically. Today, articulated lorries can load animals on two decks and transport them anywhere in the country the same day. In 1913, livestock could only be bought or sold at local markets by droving them on foot. At this time, neighbouring farmers would drove cattle for sale together on foot from their respective herds to the local market five miles away in Shepton Mallet. If any animals were purchased, they would work together again on foot to bring them home.

At the time when war broke out in 1914, agriculture in Britain had largely been neglected by the government since the agricultural depression in the 1870s. Whilst the British Empire flourished and goods travelled unhindered back to Britain, this was not a problem for the government. Eighty per cent of wheat was imported which meant only one loaf in five was made using home-grown wheat. In addition, most sugar (half of which came from Germany pre-war), lard, cheese, bacon, and condensed milk was imported and consumed by those on lower incomes. Fresh milk and meat was expensive to produce and expensive to buy so cheap imports had become a staple of the diet for those on lower incomes. With government and consumers able to enjoy cheap and plentiful imports, farmers turned to producing alternative foods, and in particular dairy and beef which provided a better income than wheat.

When war broke out on 5th August 1914, this laissez-faire policy by the government was set to change. Despite the outbreak of war, the Asquith government initially continued to import food. As trade routes with Europe became disrupted, however, focus turned to trading with old colonial allies elsewhere. Cheaper imported sugar and chilled meat flowed in from South America, Australasia, Canada and the United States by sea.

Farming cycles are long term and habits in the rural community can be slow to change. It took the government time to alter farming production, especially as predictions in August 1914 were that it 'would all be over by Christmas'. Government calls to plough up land to grow arable crops with lower returns initially went unheeded while high levels of cheap imports still poured in. Tilling the land was labour-intensive too, and the departure of land workers and horses for the war prolonged this reluctance.

2. A Letter from the Drawer

The Dorothy Bag did not supply us with the first example of Allen's writing. Back when I was studying the First World War poets during my A levels, my parents had shown me a letter they possessed, kept in their drawer written by Allen to his younger brother, Jim, my grandfather. At the time of the letter, my grandfather was aged nine and boarding at Hilworth High School in Shepton Mallet. Despite the old market town being only a short distance away, Jim and his older sister, Elsie, boarded there for thirteen weeks at a time.

Allen was fifteen years old and the war had been going on now for over a year. It had not all been over by Christmas after all. He had left school and was working at home on the farm. The letter is beautifully hand written in black ink and shows a loving warmth between the two brothers.

Hilworth High School
Shepton Mallet
Nov 15th 1915

My Dear Jim

I am sorry I did not write to you before. Eddie came home last Saturday week, he came up and spent a couple of hours with us on Sunday afternoon. He said that he did not want to go out in France again. He told me that he came in and saw you one afternoon. I think he is looking very well.

One day I went out with my gun and shot another hare. Mr Crees came over on Thursday shooting, we only shot a few rabbits, it was rather wet.

On Sunday afternoon Uncle Alf and Auntie Pollie, Tom and Jack came up and stayed until night. We have church now at 5 o'clock. It is rather early for us now. I think Mother is coming in to see you in about two weeks time. Lilly went last Saturday night. I drove her down when I took the milk down. Her Father does not get much better.

I am glad to have a letter from you, hoping that you and Elsie are quite well. Mother and Dad are also alright. Now I must close with love

from Allen

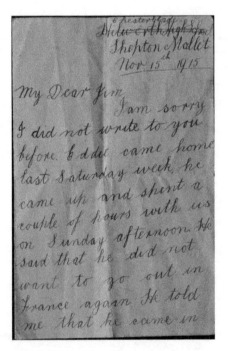

Allen's letter to his younger brother in 1915

My father has recounted to me how my grandfather hated being away from home for thirteen weeks at a time, so he would have cherished this letter from his brother. The length of time does seem slightly absurd when the school was only four miles away. Maybe it's some form of genetic masochistic trait the Greens have, as I too was sent off to a nearby boarding school in a neighbouring market town, although I did get off relatively lightly as I was allowed home once a month for a weekend!

The letter is one of the few surviving pieces of evidence we have which gives us a window into Allen's pre-war life at this time. It shines light on a time when people would spend time visiting each other as a recreational activity. It was almost a duty to visit your family elders on a Sunday night. Even in my lifetime, I remember as a child how my aunts and uncles would take it in turn on Sunday evenings to come and visit my grandfather, Jim, who was now an ageing family patriarch. It was almost like a scene from *The Godfather*, with the lower ranked underlings treading in softly to his chambers to kiss his hand in deference. My father also speaks of how he had to go and visit his grandparents, Sidney and Mabel, and it was very much a moment to be 'seen and not heard' and only 'speak when you're spoken to'. He describes his grandmother as *'someone who had swollen feet, walked with a stick, and always had a bottle of gin to hand'*.

Another insight into Allen's life before the war is glimpsed in a farm sale catalogue dated 7 November 1916. Throughout the catalogue are a series of pencilled drawings and ditties that would probably have been scribbled down as the sale progressed slowly through the different lots. You get the impression Allen is probably sitting next to his younger brother, Jim, who would have been aged nine.

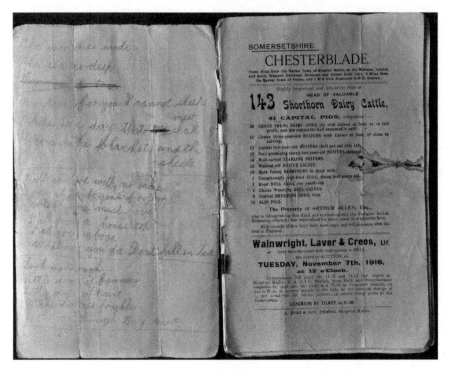

1916 sale catalogue

On the inside front cover, Allen, aged seventeen, has written:

> 'The world is wide
> The sea is deep
> My love, for you, I cannot sleep
> I hope some day that we shall meet
> Between the blankets and the sheets.'

Another reads:
'Fall in love with no man
Even if it be your brother.

Girls, if you must love
Fall from a house top
Fall from above
Whatever you do. Don't fall in love.'

And one more:
'Little drop of brandy
Little dab of paint
Make Ladies freckles
Look as though they aint.'

At the top of two pages in the middle of the catalogue the two brothers have each written their names. On the inside back cover Allen has scribbled an ode to his brother:

'Jimmy Green is a fool
Like a monkey on a stool
When the stool began to break
All the fleas went up Jim's back.'

One more ditty to love finishes off the farm sale catalogue poetry entries:
'Love is like a mutton chop
Sometimes cold and sometimes hot.'

The catalogue itself related to the sale of Arthur Allen's one hundred and forty-three head Shorthorn dairy herd in Chesterblade at Manor Farm. He had decided to continue solely with his pedigree British Holstein dairy herd instead of the mixed herds, which was very much a sign of the times as traditional native cattle were losing favour to breeds from the continent that produced more milk. In this time of war, the catalogue notes '*All the Young Stock have been bred on the Farms, excepting two heifers purchased at the Shepton Mallet British Farmers' Red Cross Sale, 1915, and the proceeds of these two heifers will be given to the same fund*'.

3. The Consequences of the War

With the onset of war in 1914, life started to change. The first *Shepton Mallet Journal* after war is declared in August 1914 reports *'The Government have taken over control of the Railways, and are assuming responsibility for food distribution. The Banks throughout the country, which have been closed since last Saturday, will re-open this morning when £1 and £10 notes will be issued to compensate for the shortness of gold.'*

Forthcoming local agricultural events and flower shows were cancelled, including the Frome District Agricultural Show, which still takes place every September today. Local newspapers warned shoppers against panic buying as scarcity would assist the enemy, although this seemed to go unheeded as reports described how shoppers had begun to stockpile.

War relief committees and fund raising groups were established in the area, such as a local branch of the National Herb Growing Association to *'encourage the growing and collecting of herbs for medicinal and other purposes, and thus become independent of the markets of Central Europe'.* The Frome Fanciers Association organised the collection of eggs in the area to supply the temporary hospitals that were established. This became so successful that they eventually also helped supply hospitals nationally. Local school children also collected for the Red Cross Hospitals various vegetables, fruit, nuts and jams. Conkers were also collected by the children and used in the manufacture of acetone for munitions.

Civilian forces and boys' organisations were mobilised to be on guard in the area against acts of espionage and spying by undercover enemy personnel, which must have added to a sense of fear and paranoia. Reservoirs in the area at Egford, Downhead and Leigh-on-Mendip were guarded by Boy Scouts and Naval Cadets. Vigilance was in the air as newspaper articles urged their readers to look out for 'suspicious persons'.

But whilst there was a degree of paranoia towards foreigners, the need to help refugees from the German invasion in mainland Europe was embraced. The Frome Refugee Committee organised to take in fifty of the million or so Belgians that had been displaced from their homes. Refugees from Antwerp and Ostend were welcomed on arrival at Frome train station in September 1914. A Flemish translator recounted to a local newspaper their horrific stories of friends and relatives shot in cold blood, and homes looted and burnt.

In November 1914, around seven hundred men arrived in Frome as part of the Royal Field Artillery camp that was to be based in the town. The recruits would stay here for twelve weeks of training before being sent to war and numbers stationed at the camp eventually swelled to around three thousand men. The War Office requisitioned as many vacant buildings as it could in the town to house officers near to the open land where the main camp was based.

Somerset endured heavy rainfall throughout December 1914 resulting in extensive flooding. Snowstorms and further torrential rain on the Monday after Christmas must have made for a down-hearted Christmas period given the war situation. Local towns such as Frome and Shepton Mallet became severely flooded and the farm land would have been underwater in many parts. This would have been more difficult than today to cope with for farm animals. Most animals were out-wintered in fields as large farm sheds were not yet in existence. Further severe storms of this magnitude were also reported to have drenched the area in May 1917, causing major flooding again.

The local foundry in Frome, J. W. Singer and Sons Ltd, was requisitioned by the government who converted the premises into munitions production and the Market Hall in the town was used as a foundry to make shell cases and fuses, employing seven hundred people. As male workers became scarce, women began to undertake work previously only done by men. The working environment was dirty, noisy and dangerous, with reports of numerous accidents and loss of limbs. Temporary hospitals also began to spring up around the area with two in Frome and one nearby at Longleat House. Around three thousand beds were created in Somerset alone by the Red Cross.

As industry took up a pivotal role producing munitions, farming became vital to feed the nation as trade routes became cut off by German U-Boats at a time when Britain was only forty per cent self-sufficient in food. A turning point came in August 1916 when bad weather caused a terrible harvest which left the nation with only six weeks of wheat supply. North America and Canada also suffered a bad harvest and these two countries, up until this point, had accounted for fifty per cent of wheat imports. With trade routes blocked, this became a crisis and brought the impact of the war closer to home for many. Germany now ramped up the pressure to try and starve Britain into submission. In September 1916, German U-Boat activity increased, reducing sugar imports by almost twenty per cent and potatoes by sixteen per cent. These two foods were the staples of the nation's diet at the time and food prices and inflation rose in the shops. So in October 1916, the Royal Commission on Wheat Supply was created and with it a philosophy that crops could supply more human food per acre than livestock for meat production was able to. Figures at the time suggested that one hundred acres of wheat could feed two hundred and eight people with bread for a year, but one hundred acres of pasture could only feed forty people with beef and mutton for a year. Local committees visited farms in the area to decide which fields should be ploughed up.

With the war now seemingly sinking into long term attrition and food supply becoming an issue, December 1916 saw a new Lloyd George coalition government installed, and with it a change in government food policy from 'horn to corn'. Prior to the war, livestock production was the dominant home sector over corn production but now stimulants were given to the arable sector.

Guaranteed prices for wheat and oats were introduced and milk production was prioritised over meat production in the allocation of scarce resources, such as feedstuffs. A Food Controller was appointed to manage and intervene when necessary in the network of food distribution. The War Cabinet also announced that no more full-time agricultural labourers would be called up to fight without the consent of the County Executive Committee, and as such, agriculture now had the same level of protection as mining and munitions as food supply had reached crisis point.

German attacks in the Atlantic became effective in 1917 with one in four Allied ships sunk. This piled pressure on food supplies so a voluntary code of rationing was introduced in 1917, and households were fined for wasting food that was 'fit to eat'. The code also suggested no more than two courses for lunch and three courses for supper when dining publicly. More than one hundred and seventy thousand men who worked on the land, about a third of the workforce, were sent to war and around half of the one million horses working on farms were requisitioned for the war effort, so farms had to adapt to new ways of working.

The British Army already had around twenty-five thousand horses, mainly for cavalry use. The horses requisitioned from farms were mainly used for logistical support and their previous work over farming ground stood them in good stead for their new role. An Army Act in 1881 had given the military emergency powers to requisition horses and carriages from the general population. In 1887, the Remount Department became responsible for carrying this out when required and had developed a scheme whereby owners had to register their horses with the authorities. As part of the Army Service Corps, in 1914 the War Office sent agents from the Remount Department out across the country to requisition horses that were now required for the war effort. As the mechanisation of war reduced the importance of the cavalry, the horses in demand were the draft horses. 'Draft' came from the Old English word 'dragan', which meant 'to draw or haul'.

> **EXTRAORDINARY**
> **SCENE IN THE SALE YARD.**
> **OVER 1,000 HORSES.**
> **PROMPT GOVERNMENT PAYMENT.**
> The call upon the horse owners of the district was so freely responded to that well over a thousand horses it was estimated were submitted for inspection yesterday (Thursday) morning, at the sale yard of Messrs. Wainwright, Laver and Crees. A great many of these were returned with their owners, but many selections were made. It was stated that those whose horses were taken on Wednesday received Government cheques for them on Thursday morning.

Shepton Mallet Journal 7 August 1914

On the first market day after war had been declared in 1914, War Office agents arrived at the market in the nearby town of Frome to requisition horses, whether they were registered or not, for the fee of £40 if they passed the medical examination by vets brought in for the day. Most horse owners patriotically handed over their horses to the cause; especially as they believed the war would be of short duration. They then had to find alternative means of getting home that day. Others were more reticent in the knowledge that the work of the horses would be integral to the fast-approaching harvest. Twenty-three horses were requisitioned in Frome, with another thirty-three rejected as not medically sound. The following day, the agents travelled around the area requisitioning more horses. In Shepton Mallet, the Journal reported a thousand horses being inspected by government agents at the local market.

The army also recognised the strong bond that existed between a man and his horse so advertised for recruits between the age of twenty-five and forty to join the Army Remount Department, but warned '*Only men thoroughly accustomed to horses required*'. The noise and explosions of a war-zone must have been terrifying for the animals and the death rate for horses was high. They would suffer from diseases like mud fever as well as wounds from artillery and shrapnel. The loss of a horse was also a huge tactical set back, and as losses grew and the supply of replacement horses from England dried up, the government started bringing in horses from across the Atlantic to help the war effort.

Moving horse fodder to the front line for half a million horses was a massive logistical operation and this was the single biggest commodity shipped during the war. A poor Italian harvest and increasingly effective German submarine attacks on oat shipments from North America in 1917 put pressure on feeding the horses and even they had to go onto rationing. This was the last war in which horses were used on any kind of scale and it also prompted the beginning of their demise for farm work. The war accelerated a new age of mechanisation that would replace both horses and people on the farm.

At the beginning of the war, British farming was already the most mechanised in Europe with field operations such as corn harvesting, grass mowing and hay making long since undertaken with the use of machinery, but still mostly in conjunction with horses. Dairy was less mechanised than the arable sector, with most cows still milked by hand. Around eighty thousand cows were being mechanically milked at this time and experiments were taking place to increase the efficiency and availability of this method. When livestock farmers were told by the government to plough up their pasture land to grow crops, they didn't have knowledge of large scale arable production and farmers in general didn't know how to use these new machines, as horses were the mainstay of production. There were also delays in the distribution of fertilisers and feedstuffs due to the war effort and the soldiers, civilians and prisoners of war drafted in to help weren't always as adept or efficient at the farm work as the skilled workers away in the war.

The Board of Agriculture started running training courses in farm based work for women at agricultural colleges in 1915 due to the lack of labour available to undertake farm work. The courses lasted twenty-five weeks and focused on 'light' farm work and milking. Two hundred and eighteen women signed up and one hundred and ninety eight found work afterwards. The training wasn't very effective, however, so many organised themselves into their own associations to find work. In September 1915, the Womens' Institute was also formed and held its first meeting in Wales. This all helped lead on to ninety-eight thousand women becoming part of the Woman's Land Army in 1917. Its aims were recruitment, breaking down anti-feminine bias and organising women into work gangs. In the fields the women wore leather gaiters to protect their legs, rubber coats in wet weather, and a broad brimmed hat with the WLA badge on. For indoor work, long heavy cotton coats were worn to keep them clean. To demonstrate their contribution to the war effort, after thirty days of farm work the women were entitled to wear a military styled armband. By 1918, around two hundred and sixty thousand women were working in agriculture, twenty-three thousand of whom were in the WLA. The others were women who already worked on farms anyway or women in the family who stepped in when the men left the farm and went off to war.

A Woman's Land Army uniform in the Imperial War Museum, London

When seasonal work was at its busiest, soldiers with knowledge and experience of operating steam ploughs and soldiers on leave were called back to the farms to help. In total, around sixty-six thousand soldiers returned home to help out at harvest time. Moving the clocks forward an hour for British Summer Time was first instituted in 1916 to extend the working hours available in agriculture.

Before 1914 there were less than one thousand tractors in the country. Now, steam engine ploughing sets were used alongside the tried and trusted horses, or to replace the horses that had gone to war. By 1917, however, around half the steam engines were lying idle due to a lack of mechanics, spare parts, coal and skilled labour to operate them. During the conflict, the prices of machinery and spare parts rose by around fifty per cent, due to a lack of blacksmiths available to undertake repairs. Motor tractors were still in their infancy but four hundred British Saunderson tractors were purchased by the government in 1917 and seven hundred and thirty thousand pounds (the equivalent of forty-eight million pounds today) were invested in American Fordson tractors. There were shipping difficulties and delays and some US models were found to be unsuitable for land conditions in this country, with reports of tractors tipping over on uneven ground. All the machines had iron wheels, backfired a lot and had to be started by hand with a crank handle. There are reports of many accidents and arms being broken as the machines were dangerous. By the end of the war, however, six thousand tractors were used on the land and without all this increased mechanisation, the 'Ploughing Up' government campaign in 1917, that resulted in two and a half million extra acres of land being ploughed up for cereals, would not have been possible.

Today, when we are bemoaning the difficulties of harvesting a crop or getting the next crop planted before it rains, it's good to stop and consider the difficulties faced a hundred years ago in keeping food supplies going. If it was difficult in England, it was even harder in the war zones of France. Here is an extract from the *Shepton Mallet Journal* on 15 November 1918:

FOOD IN FRANCE
How Our Army Saves It
BY LIEUT. K. N. COLVILLE

The Agricultural Directorate of the British Army in France has had a hard time of it this year. Hardly had it arranged for the sowing of its spring crops when the Germans advanced over the seed beds. Then, in the middle of the summer, the invaders had to retire, and the Directorate was called on to harvest the crops which the enemy had had time neither to reap nor destroy. But, in spite of the difficulty making and carrying out its schemes which the varying fortunes of the war have caused, a great deal of food has been produced by the Army, and a great deal of transport, as well as public money has thereby been saved. The Army benefited, moreover, for by no other means could it have been so well supplied with fresh vegetables.

The scale on which the Directorate works is considerable. By March 21st, twenty thousand acres had been prepared, the work being done by low grade men, specially recruited or drawn from Labour Battalions, with a couple hundred tractors and a number of Canadian three furrow ploughs, each tractor ploughing an average of three to four acres a day. All this alas! was, as it proved, labour lost, although the tractors themselves were saved.

But the Allies' counter-offensive gave an opportunity of harvesting the crops in a large area which the French civilians had had to evacuate, and the British Army can thus claim the credit of getting in from twenty to thirty thousand acres of wheat and oats, which would otherwise never have been harvested in time. On many acres, we are told, the crops were actually scythed and carried under shell fire, and some even had to be cut by night, to avoid the direct observation of the enemy. Besides the work for which the Directorate was wholly responsible, troops at rest were freely lent to the French farmers in areas where they themselves could take charge of the work.

Now, with the much larger area reclaimed, the Directorate has the huge task before it to clean, work, and manure the soil in what was lately the battle-zone. About forty thousand acres are already under cultivation, directly managed either by the Directorate or by the agriculture officers of the armies, divisions, and lines of communication. Thousands of tons of manure have been collected. The best Scotch and English seeds have been obtained, and vegetables are being sown in nurseries at various bases for transplanting into the forward areas. Even by the end of July, nearly two and a half million pounds of fresh vegetables had been supplied by the Army in this scheme, although the Directorate was only established at the end of 1917.

PART THREE
LETTERS FROM THE PAST

1. Wyke Regis - 2017

In the autumn of 2017, I decided to track down the site of Allen's army camp base at Wyke Regis while I was on holiday in the area. The centenary of his time in the Great War in 1918 would be the following year and his story kept calling to me. Wyke Regis sits to the west of Weymouth, across the water, tucked in behind the lagoon created by the seemingly never ending stretch of Chesil Beach. I didn't know its exact location but noticed there was a road called Camp Road on the map and figured this could be it.

I mused to myself about the differences between then and now; how different Allen's life would have been to mine, yet still so similar when it comes to farming the land; how I can track down his camp location with a hand held electronic device; how much more traffic there is now; how the roads he cycled on and the landscape he lived in differed from my experience. The previous day, I had taken a steam train (a relic of a bygone age operated as a tourist attraction) from Corfe Castle to Swanage. In 1917 these trains were moving troops and munitions around, and were a crucial part of the war effort. The local museums tell of how sections of track were pulled up and taken across to France to aid the movement of soldiers and munitions to the front.

My mind snapped back to the modern day task in hand as my soft-voiced Irish sat-nav companion instructed me to turn off left into Camp Road. I had just driven through Weymouth and had my childhood memories of the town (a bit of a dump back then) jolted. It now looked very different, having undergone the same gentrification that Somerset market towns have witnessed in the last few years.

As my car nudged down into Camp Road, I felt a strange thrill as a chain link fence topped with coils of razor wire come into view on my right. This must be it. I stopped in the road alongside the fence and felt a bolt of connection to Allen and his life here. A faded red and white sign half-obscured with ivy read:

ARMY ROAD

PUBLIC BRIDLE PATH

VEHICLES PROCEED AT OWNERS RISK

A tired-looking road trailed off to the right along the fence line and I drove slowly down it. The rusting fence line appeared to go all around the site which was the size of around six football pitches and sloped down towards the sea. Periodic signs attached to the chain link warned of guard dogs and prosecution. Inside the fence, brambles and briars sprawled between patches of rough grassland, crumbling tarmac and concrete. Various tin, wood, and brick huts sat scattered with broken asbestos roofs and smashed-in windows. It was hard to believe that Allen's old encampment still existed.

At the end of the road along the top edge of the base, there appeared an industrial warehouse selling builders' materials, although the gates were padlocked shut. On the corner, a gravel track with rain filled potholes followed down alongside to the right of the fence towards the sea. At the bottom a hundred yards from the lagoon, miserable looking windblown ponies stood in mud pocked paddocks on a shabby looking small holding. Small stacks of black plastic covered fodder bales sat plump as sacks stranded between patches of brambles. The wind had blown large pieces of plastic from them onto the razor wire in random places around the site perimeter.

The site in Wyke Regis where Allen's army camp was based

I got out of the car to take it all in and the wind gusting off the sea hit me. The late October skies were grey and damp, and the threat of rain blew in the air. I took out my phone and started to take photos through the wire. A lady walking a dog tramped along the gravel track towards me and I was conscious I was taking photos of an army base. I tried to seem normal by asking her if this was the old army camp and explained its connection to my great uncle. She confirmed it was but said it was recently sold off to a private buyer who wanted to build houses on the site. The local council denied him permission so he then threatened to turn it into a travellers' site. An impasse now existed with the only activity being infrequent car boot sales. I wondered to myself where they could set up their lines of cars amongst the brambles and how they stop the wind blowing everything off the tables.

Our gaze returned to the old camp. The lady pointed out a collection of broken concrete slabs amongst the overgrown grass in the top corner, near where we stood. This was where the soldiers' tents were located during the First World War. It was such a strange feeling to be standing there imagining the scene. Imagining Allen's sudden change of life away from the farm in Somerset to that army camp on a windblown hillside looking down to the lagoon, Chesil Beach, the open sea and a war-torn France, where he would soon be going to fight Germans much like himself.

2. A POSTCARD

The next item out of Allen's Dorothy bag, following the letter from Wyke Regis confirming that he had been conscripted into the army, was a postcard. It read:

25.6.1918

Dear Mother,

I received my letter and parcel today. Could you send on a small blacking tin and cash box without the tilt and put it in a little salt bag. Then I can send back my dirty clothes in it. I do not want any socks. Hope you are quite all right and haymaking going.

From Allen

3. Wyke Regis - 2017

The lady went on to point out some newer buildings that buffered the lagoon, below Allen's old encampment and beyond the pony paddocks. The army were still based here and used this area, she said, as a bridging camp for training. Unlike its untidy counterparts, higher up the hill, these fences were newer, less rusty, and all stood to attention. A handful of men could be seen moving between buildings and loading a truck but otherwise it seemed deserted. You could almost feel the ghosts of soldiers past watching down on them from the abandoned camp above.

The entrance to Pebble Beach caravan park opposite Allen's old army camp

I wanted to stay as close as possible to the camp, to get inside Allen's experience, and asked the lady if there was anywhere to stay close by. She pointed me in the direction of a caravan park called Pebble Beach on the other side of the army camp. As I headed back to Camp Road I saw the park directly across the road. It looked just as deserted as the old camp; they almost seemed to co-exist on the windblown hillside together like comrades. It seemed like the perfect place to stay.

I parked up next to a row of caravans with 'Bordeaux' written on them. Stunted trees had been blown crooked at forty five degrees. I walked into the reception area to enquire about staying the night and became aware that I probably looked a bit of an odd proposition to behold; a middle-aged man wanting to stay on his own in a half deserted family caravan holiday park in late October for one night. Luckily for me, the middle-aged lady in reception seemed amused by the absurdity of my request.

'The minimum is a two-night stay.'

I asked if there were any caravans free if I stayed for two nights. The place seemed deserted so I was guessing she would be glad of some custom. Hurricane Brian had been threatening the shores of the UK over the last week and although it was half term, the park felt shut down for the winter already.

'B5 is free. It will be two hundred and forty pounds for the two nights.'

This seemed a bit steep for a caravan on a windy slope in late October.

'Could I have a quick look first?'

She handed me a key and pointed me in the direction of a caravan with a prime view of the car park. A handmade wooden step had been pushed to the left of the door into the caravan, just under a name plate that read 'Elegance'. I pushed the step back in line with the doorway but the paving below was uneven and too high for the door to open, so I pushed it back to its original off-set location, unlocked the door and balanced a foot on the side of the step to go in. The inside looked brand new, as if no-one had stayed there before, and it was perfectly adequate for my needs. In my twenties, I lived in a caravan on the farm for seven years before building a house, so I was well used to living like this.

I called back down to the reception area to see the lady.

'All looks fine to me.' I didn't mention the step as I was reluctant to be seen as a troublemaker as well as odd. 'Is there any chance you could do a discount at all as it seems a lot for a caravan for one person?'

'Sorry, love. I'd have to ask the owner and she's not here at the moment.'

I decided to have a quick drive around the area, to see if there might be a better place to stay. I noticed a sign for the Albert Inn, leading off the main road down into Wyke Regis and headed for this. After travelling through a couple of drab-looking streets, I came across the inn. It had a peeling façade, dirty boarded up windows and a For Sale sign displayed in one of them. Driving on a little further, I came across a farmhouse bed and breakfast near to the lagoon edge with caravan and camping spaces and pulled into the yard where there were two scruffy alpacas in a windswept, muddy paddock. There were no other inhabitants around. I decided to keep going.

Next, I came across a house that looked like a small castle and I wondered if this might be a hotel. It wasn't, but it was at the top of Pirates Lane which headed off down towards the sea and I spied caravans in the distance so decided to investigate. Tarmac quickly degenerated into a rutted track and as I got closer I realised this might not be holiday accommodation. A sign on a chain link fence with barbed wire along the top read:

> *YOU ARE NOW ENTERING*
> *PIRATES' COVE LAND*
> *AT YOUR OWN RISK*

Behind the fence dozens of shabby caravans, shepherds' huts, vans, and sheds sat defiantly amongst vegetable allotments. I presumed this was the travellers' camp that they'd proposed should be sited at the old army camp. No-one was around. In any case, there was no bed for the night. Across the lagoon on the facing bank of Chesil Beach, a handful of fishermen's huts sat rusting. Like everything else along this windblown stretch, they seemed abandoned, so I turned the car around and headed back up the track.

When I headed back to the first caravan park, it was hard to tell if the lady was pleased to see me again but she phoned the owner at my request and got me a discount after all.

'I noticed the beds weren't made up earlier. Could someone look in and sort me out with sheets?'

'Sorry, love. You have to bring your own linen and towels here.'

After explaining the spontaneity of my stay she ferreted around for some spare linen nonetheless and handed me a towel that was about a foot square.

'Here's some linen but I'm afraid that's the only towel I've got in the cupboard.' She smiled apologetically but seemed pleased to have risen to the challenge.

Despite the strangeness, a half-deserted caravan park next to Allen's old base seemed perfect to try and imagine what the camp would have been like. The view was pretty much the same as a hundred years ago. The sea still crashed into Chesil Beach just the same and the wind still blew the sea mist hard in your face. I decided to stay on for the two days to take it all in. It was getting cold so I put the heating on and went to the bathroom, only to find no toilet roll (of course) and no heating as the gas bottles were empty.

Feeling like a definite pest, I went down to the reception again.

'Sorry, love. You have to bring your own loo rolls here. Probably best to go up to the shower block and pinch some paper from the toilets up there.

I'll get our handyman to sort you out with some gas later.'

Unperturbed, I went back up to my shack on the hill via a loo roll raid on the shower block. A while later, a paint-splattered man with a Scouse accent and bleached blond surfer hair came over and sorted out the gas. He seemed out of place here. There was no sun, no surf and I wonder where his tan had come from. It can't have been from there, or north-west England. He was, however, cheerful and amiable and I made a silent prayer on his behalf that he might end up somewhere hot with great waves. I noticed the caravan next door was called 'Brisbane' and wondered if that was where he lived.

Not long afterwards, I went for a walk to take a closer look at Allen's camp and document my time there with photos. It seemed important to do this before the new owners covered it with travellers, car boot sales or houses. Taking the coastal path in an easterly direction towards Portland, poor grassland buffered the lagoon from habitation and I passed dog walkers dressed for winter, gamely throwing sticks.

As darkness descended, I headed back to the caravan park restaurant, the Fat Badger. I came to love the deserted feel of the place over the next two nights. In total, there were around a dozen of us mooching around the place, including the staff, like a band of apocalypse survivors. A strange camaraderie bound us together against the climate and circumstances. It had been a perfect introduction to Allen's desolate hillside camp.

I tried to imagine him bunked up with eleven other conscripted farmers' sons in a tent a few hundred yards away from the, by comparison, luxury mobile home. That people now choose to come here and pitch up on the same hillside for pleasure seemed an irony.

4. A Letter Home

29.6.1918

No 42915
A Company
3rd Dorsets Regt
Smallmouth Camp,
Wyke Regis
Nr Weymouth

Dear Mother,

I received my parcels quite safe yesterday Friday. Those gooseberries were lovely and the ham I shall have for my supper but do not send any more cheese before I want it. I am glad you have got a girl and hope she will do. Also I am glad to hear that you are getting on with the haymaking. I should like to see Jim up in the tedder and telling the pony to go in his sleep. I'll bet he is so pleased as punch. I should have thought Mr Allen had plenty of land now without buying any more. Will you tell Mr Crees not to come and see me before I tell you because the whole camp have got bad colds, and half of them are on the sick. So we are not aloud (sic) out of camp and nobody can come and see us because of spreading the disease. I have had one but its better now and a good job too. I shall be glad when the restrictions are took off. I shall send home my dirty clothes at the end of next week. I think the photos are come out well. Tell John that I seen Harold Meek the other day. We have half day Saturday and only church parade Sunday. I do call soldier life is a lazy life.

(missing page as no signing off).

From this letter, it seems, a land girl has now joined the farm at home to help out as Allen's exemption from conscription was 'conditional until a substitute is found'. My grandfather, Jim, although only eleven years old, would also now be stepping up to fill the gap left by Allen.

The Mr Allen in the letter refers to Arthur Allen who farmed in Chesterblade at Manor Farm and owned three other houses and cottages in the village to house farm workers. As a bachelor, Arthur Allen was knocked down by a bull and injured. Whilst in hospital recovering from his serious injuries, he met his wife to be who was a nurse in the hospital. They became well known for driving around the area together in a horse and trap.

I'm impressed that sending food parcels and washing backwards and forwards between home and the camp seemed to be relatively easy. The distance is around fifty miles and today takes around an hour and a half to drive in a car. I'm not sure our postal service is much better now than it was back then.

It's not surprising to hear of illness around the camp as the conditions were cramped and the climate, I can attest, is cold and damp on that hillside. Staying in a tent with eleven other people with varying degrees of illness would have been a challenge in itself. Spanish Flu, an influenza pandemic, was beginning to sweep the world, and is estimated to have killed between three and six per cent of the global population by the time it receded after the war. Countless more survived but endured much pain and suffering through it. Local schools in Somerset closed for five weeks and workplaces struggled to keep going due to the number of ill absentees.

Allen would have had to successfully pass an eyesight test and medical examination to be declared fit for duty. New recruits had to swear an oath to *'faithfully defend His Majesty, His Heirs and successors ... against all enemies'* and obey the authority of *'all Generals and Officers set over me'* for the entirety of the war. When Allen left the farm behind, the army now controlled his life. He had to learn military discipline, how to drill, and how to fight with a rifle and bayonet. In his recollections of the camp at Wyke Regis, Allen's friend Cary wrote *'we often had to march the length of Chesil Beach before breakfast, much to the disgust of several townies who were not used to doing anything before breakfast'*. Chesil Beach is eighteen miles long. The camp would have been a mixture of wooden huts and tents, and men from all walks of life would have come together here in often cramped conditions, though the West Country base at Wyke Regis would have had many farmers' sons. Officers were usually recruited from universities and public schools. More than one hundred and seventy thousand farmers fought in the trenches.

The coming together of men in camps inevitably had some knock on effects for the surrounding area. Pregnancy rates and arrests for drunkenness rose around the camps and extra facilities like public toilets had to be introduced to cope with the influx.

For many young men, the camp would be their first time away from home and for most, going to France would be their first time abroad. Their pay book carried a message from Lord Kitchener instructing the soldier to be *'courteous, considerate and kind'* to local people and allied soldiers, and to avoid *'the temptations both in wine and women'*.

5. A Letter to his Sister

5.7.1918

No 42915 A Company 3rd dorsets
Smallmouth Camp,
Wyke Regis, Near Weymouth

Dear Elsie,

I have sent on my dirty clothes tonight. When you send back the clean, could you put in a flannel, 2 old dusters and an old medicine bottle not too big. So I can keep some oil in to clean my rifle with. I received my parcel alright, and must thank you very much for it especially for the cake.

(missing page)

Ps How is the haymaking getting on. Did T. Witcombe come and see Dad.

6. A Postcard Home

6.7.1918

Dear Mother,

Will you put my other vest in when you send back my clean clothes. I forgot to tell you when I wrote to Elsie. I received the Journal today. Am writing this in a restaurant in Weymouth having some tea.

With love from Allen

Looking back through the newspaper archives of the *Shepton Mallet Journal*, which is still going strong today, the front page for 28 June 1918, which is probably the edition Allen received in the post from Elsie, gives a fascinating snapshot of the times. A front page advertisement states that for £250, farmers can now order a Fordson tractor that *'displaces three or four horses on the farm and enormously extends the possibilities of agricultural production'*. Ironically, the advertisement directly below this one is for a coachbuilder, wheelwright and blacksmith; all the skills that the tractor will displace completely and put out of business in the not too distant future. On another page, articles give tips and advice regarding making the best use of food in the age of wartime rationing and other related topics. Home grown vegetables will have kept many families going as food became increasingly scarce and expensive. Other articles include the best way to conserve vegetables going into the winter, the price of milk, how to deal with cabbage butterfly pest, and recipe ideas.

Shepton Mallet Journal 28 June 1918

7. A Postcard Home post marked Sunday 14ᵀᴴ July

Dear Mother,

Will you send my other vest so I can send back my dirty one. Can you put in quarter lb of butter, put it in a cup then it will not be all over the place. Here is a nice drop of rain, I suppose it will make the grass grow a bit. How is the corn looking? I had my photo taken last night in Weymouth. I have seen H. Treasure he will soon be going to France. Hope the family are alright as it leaves me the same.

The photo taken in Weymouth mentioned here will probably have been the photograph of Allen in his army uniform that my parents still have at home in the drawer.

8. An Undated Letter Home

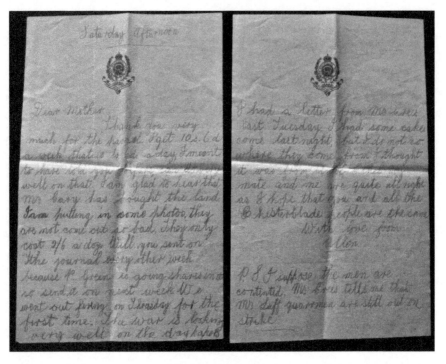

One of Allen's letters home

Saturday afternoon

Dear Mother,

Thank you very much for the parcel. I get 10s 6d a week that is 1s 6d a day, I meant to have told you before, I can do very well on that. I am glad to hear Mr Cary has bought the land. I am putting in some photos, they are not come out so bad. They only cost 2/6 a dozen. Will you send on the Journal every other week because P. Green is going shares in it so send it on next week. We went out firing on Thursday for the first time. The war is looking very well on the day papers.
I had a letter from Mr Crees last Tuesday. I had some cakes come last night, but I do not know where they come from. I thought it was from Auntie Ethel. My mate and me are quite all right as I hope that you and all the Chesterblade people are the same.
With love from, Allen
P.S. I suppose the men are contented. Mr Crees tells me that Mr Luffs quarrymen are still out on strike.

(with the same letter)

Dear Jim,

I received your letter quite alright and the parcel that Mother sent and must thank you very much for it. I suppose you are getting a big man with the horses now. I am surprised to hear that old Ted is leaving Mr Allen, will you let me know the reason why? I suppose the pigs are good ones by now. It is a pity the ferret is not in young. I reckon that you were lucky to finish haymaking and done up all the ricks before all this rain. I hope we do not get too much of it, will be bad for the harvest. It will not make a difference about here because there is not much arable.

Has grandfather started ploughing poison ground yet. I am glad to hear P. Butler has not heard any more about army, tell him to keep out of it as long as he can.

I hope that all of the Aunties and Grandfather are alright and dad, Mother, Elsie and yourself. As it leaves me the same. Now I must close from your loving brother

Allen

9. A POSTCARD POST MARKED 24 JULY 1918

Dear Mother,

I had your postcard tonight. Could you send on a bit of cheese and butter with the clean clothes. I hope you will get this card before you send on the clothes. What do you think of the photos. Would you send on a photo, one taken with Jim and me. I think we are going to have some more fine weather. I suppose the corn is getting ripe. I hope you are all well as this leaves me the same.

Allen

I'm touched reading these letters and postcards, and the brotherly bond between Allen and my grandfather always comes through with love and warmth. The phrase 'I hope you are all well as it leaves me the same' sounds so poetic and conveys such a caring sentiment.

10. A Letter post marked 30 July 1918

Monday night

Dear Elsie,

I had the Journal on Saturday and the parcel alright and must thank you very much for it. I forgot to send the socks last week so I wash them out myself, I suppose you would laugh to see me, we have to do all sorts in the army. I am not going to send my dirty clothes home because there is a woman in the village is going to wash it for a 1s. It is where Percy Green sends his too and he says it is wash clean, so I thought it would be cheaper than sending it home. I have been on a route march today we went about 12 miles with our full pack, and had to where (sic) the gas masks some of the time, it was hot enough to melt anyone. I think we are going to have another fine start, I hope we shall, so Dad will be able to harvest the corn alright. Who is going with the reaper. We go on church parade every Sunday morning. We are going to have some sports next Saturday, I am in for the sack race and 100 yards.

I hope you are quite all well, as it leaves me same.

Love to you all

From Allen

It does seem a little odd, reading these letters, that the army camp doesn't seem to have any provision for washing clothes but at least now he has found someone local which will save all the backwards and forwards of dirty and clean clothes. It is probably less surprising that there isn't enough food to keep a young man going and food supplies sent from home can help with this in a time of rationing. At the beginning of 1918, sugar became rationed, followed by tea, bread, butter, margarine, cheese, and meat in April. Going without food between 4pm one day and 8am the next, as Allen described in an earlier letter, is a long time if you're undertaking lots of physical exercise during the day.

How the harvest is looking is also a hot topic at a time of food shortages and an ongoing war with German U-boats sinking ships bringing in food imports. In the 26th July 1918 edition of the *Shepton Mallet Journal* the retail prices of butter as set by the local Food Control Committee are reported. During the war, it was illegal to sell food above the prices set by the Committee to keep food affordable for everyone. Another article lists the times of day and night for the week ahead when lights have to be turned off both for vehicles and in houses due to blackout rules. It makes you realise how lucky we are today and how we take simple things for granted like food and when we turn a light on. They really were extraordinary times.

11. A Letter Home

4th August 1918

Dear Mother,

I received my parcel quite safe the other day and must thank you very much for it. Could you send the next parcel in a tin box, because it gets broke all to pieces when it sent any how else. I have not had a letter from Elsie yet. I am going to try for a weekend in a weeks time but I do not know if it is any good or not. Any one must have some good reasons to get one. The reason why Pole got a weekend was that he said that his Father was crippled and was not able to see to his business. I should like to see the corn before it is cut. I suppose it is getting ripe by now. We had some sports yesterday it went oft very well. I suppose Mrs Hill of Smalldown wished it was a son. I heard that N. Naish is a jolly sight worse than I am. I have got his address. I hope you are all quite well, as it leaves me the same. I will send home the tins and bags.

With love
From Allen

I raised an eyebrow that someone had to have a good reason to be able to visit their family before being sent off to war. That you might never come back and see them again I would have thought is reason enough.

12. A Letter Home

6th Aug Tues Night. 42915 A Company, 3rd Dorset Regt, Smallmouth Camp, Wyke Regis,
Near Weymouth

Dear Mother,

I am sending back the tins and one of the salt bags and am keeping the other one to keep a few things in. I have not had a letter yet from Elsie. You can send on a bit more butter the end of next week, the butter we have for tea is just like a lot of cart grease. The war seems to be looking better every day and a good job to. We are in our 7th week training in another 7 weeks I hope to be home or on leave. I do not expect I will be able to come now. Pole must think himself lucky in coming home. I suppose you will soon start cutting the corn. I have been vaccinated today for the second time and have to be done again. My arm does not half get stiff. I hope you are all quite well as it leaves me the same.

With love
From Allen

One thing that starts to strike me about the letters is that there were no telephones, so letters and postcards were the only way for families to communicate with their loved ones living miles away. Getting a message to someone and receiving back an answer took days. We've become so used to the immediacy of mobile phones. Even within my lifetime this has been a change. As a child at boarding school I remember making a phone call home once a week on the communal pay phone in the stairwell of the boarding house. These days, my young daughters flick messages around to dozens of people at a time to chat and make arrangements to meet up.

The series of vaccinations he received and the stiff arm are interesting. At this time, recruits were receiving injections for typhoid, tetanus and smallpox. Whatever it was, it had quite a side effect and clearly took a while to wear off.

13. A Letter to Jim

11ᵗʰ Aug 1918
No 42915 A Company 3ʳᵈ Dorsets
Smallmouth Camp,
Wyke Regis, Near Weymouth

Dear Jim,

I received your letter and the parcel which Mother sent, and must thank you very much for it. I do not know whether I shall be home next weekend. I cannot come unless I cycle. P. Green and me thought about trying it if we can hire a bicycle. Some of the chaps have cycled home further than I should. If I came I should start on Saturday dinner time and back Sunday night, it would not be very long, just to see how you are all getting on. I will let you know if I am coming or not in two days time. I had a letter from Eddy Ashford the other day, he said he did not think the war was going to last much longer. Also had one from Nelson Naish. Well Jim I suppose you will soon think about cutting the corn, they have cut most of it around here. I suppose Dad is beginning to get a good shot by now. Tell Mother I had back my washing and it was wash very clean for a 1s and I think it is cheaper than sending it home. Now I have not got much more news to tell you, hoping that you are all quite well and all the aunties and Grandfather and grandmother as it leaves me the same.

With love from your old Allen
PS I had the journal come quite safe.

Wyke Regis was fifty miles from home for Allen and today takes about one and a half hours by car, so if Allen and his mate Percy were to cycle home by bicycle it would have been quite an undertaking and shows how keen these guys were to get home and visit their families. The cycle route today would take around five hours, and this is with smooth roads and modern bicycles. Although there would have been less traffic then, the road surfaces would have been much rougher and the bicycles wouldn't have been very easy to ride like they are today with a multitude of gears and aerodynamic design. I imagine it would have taken Allen at least six hours to cycle the route one way back then.

14. A Letter Home

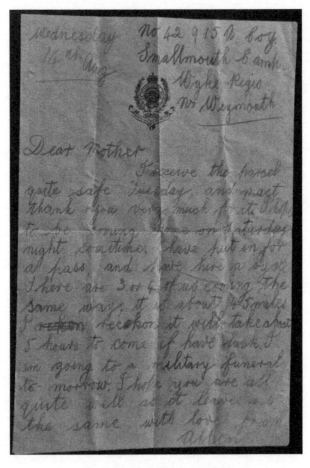

Allen's letter home 14 August 1918

14th Aug 1918
No 42915 ACoy
Smallmouth Camp,
Wyke Regis,
Nr Weymouth

Dear Mother,

I receive the parcel quite safe Tuesday and must thank you so very much for it. I hope to be coming home on Saturday night sometime. I have put in for a pass and have hired a bicycle. There are 3 or 4 of us coming in the same way, it is about 45 miles. I reckon it will take about 5 hours to come if I have luck. I am going to a military funeral tomorrow. I hope you are quite well as it leaves me the same.

With love
From Allen

So, he *did* do the mammoth cycle home after all. I can imagine having to go to a military funeral no doubt only increases the desire to see your loved ones as much as possible before going to war.

15. A Letter Home

Monday night

Dear Mother,

I have not heard from you since I receive your postcard last Tuesday. Percy Green and me thought about cycling home again next Saturday if the weather is fine and we can get a pass. I am not sure if we can get a pass or not. I will let you know later in the week if we are coming or not. I got on very well coming back last time on my own bicycle. I suppose you are busy with the corn now, when the weather is fine, it seems to be very unsettled now. The war seems to be improving every day and a good job to. I had some apricots sent me from Ditcheat last week they were very good. I have not very much news to tell this time. I hope you are all quite well as it leaves me in the best health. Now I must close,

With love
From Allen
PS. I forgot to post this letter tonight and I receive the parcel quite safe tonight Tuesday and thank you very much for it. Glad to hear Mr Allen is getting on as well as can be expected. I do not know for sure whether I am coming or not next Saturday.
From Allen

The 'Mr Allen' refers to Arthur Allen in the village who has been knocked down by a bull. Little do they all know, but this accident will lead him to meet his future wife!

16. A Letter post marked
30 August 1918

Friday

Dear Mother,

Do not be surprise to see me home tomorrow Saturday. I do not know for sure, but I do expect so. I hope you are all quite well as it leaves me the same and my arm is better now. Hope Mr Allen is getting on as well as can be expected.

With Love from Allen

The vaccination needle must have been a real stinger on 6th August for the arm to only have just stopped hurting at the end of the month.

The long cycle home and back doesn't seem to be putting Allen off from doing it again.

17. A LETTER POST MARKED 2 SEPTEMBER 1918

Monday night

Dear Mother,

I got back Sunday night quite safe about 12 o'clock. I met with three other chaps at Yeovil so we went on together. I called on Mr Weedon on my way back and they let me have Harold address, so I am going to write to him and perhaps might have a weekend at his place, it would not be very far to Dorchester. We have had a nice day today, and I suppose you are busy with the corn. I hope it will be fine for a week or two. I do not expect I will be home before I get my leave. I hope you are all quite well as it leaves me the same

With love from Allen

It seems that cycling home again, Allen met up at the halfway mark in Yeovil with some others riding back to base, finally arriving back in Wyke Regis at midnight.

The Weedons were a farming family that lived at Peking Mill where Allen grew up.

18. A Postcard dated
4 September 1918

Dear Mother,
Will you send on the Journal this week. I forgot to say anything about it when I
was home last week. I hope you are all quite well as it leaves me the same.
With love from Allen

The *Shepton Mallet Journal* of 6 September 1918 carried some interesting
notices and adverts on the second page. Coal for house fuel could only be
bought from a merchant if you had been a regular customer; the asylum
in Wells was inviting businesses to tender to supply it with beef, mutton,
coffee, chicory, rice, tobacco, soap, soda and coal. Cider, blackberries and
especially milk seemed to be in demand. One such advertisement reads
'Milk! Milk! Milk! *The Great Western and Metropolitan Dairies Ltd are now*
making their contracts for the coming winter for small or large dairies of well-
cooled milk, delivered London by any railway. Good supply of churns.'

Another, rather strange advertisement read '*Lost between Bruton and*
Shepton Mallet, a spare wheel with tyre for motor car. Finder will be rewarded.'

19. A LETTER HOME

Friday night

Dear Mother,

I received those grapes quite safe tonight Friday. I hope you will thank Mr Allen very much for me. Glad to hear he is now getting on as well as can be expected. The weather does not seem to be settled again, I wish it would hold fine so as to finish the oats. I am sending back the tin box so as you can send it back again. We are going firing Monday to Wednesday. I have not much news to tell you. Hoping you are all quite well, as it leaves me the same.

With love from Allen.

20. A Letter to Jim

Tuesday night 10th September

Dear Jim,

I receive the parcel quite safe to-night Tuesday, and the Journal last Saturday, and must thank you very much for it. Glad to hear that you have nearly hauled all the oats, the weather seems to be very unsettled at present. I suppose nearly all the odd bits of corn are hauled by now. Well Jim I suppose Grandfather was pleased with his cattle last Friday. We went on the range last Monday and fired for our pay and I pay out a first class shot, now I suppose I shall get 3d a day extra now that will be 1s 9d a day. I expect I shall go & see Harold Weedon next Saturday at Dorchester. They say we shall be at home on leave in about a fortnights time. I do not know if it is right or not. I suppose Dad went to the colt sale at Evercreech junction today. I hope you are all quite well as it leaves me the same

With love from Allen

Living on the land, Allen would have been familiar with guns and an excellent shot. Shooting hares, rabbits and wildfowl for the table was an important source of food, especially in the war years before he was drafted.

Luckily for him, this helped increase his soldier's pay, although it may also have increased his chances of frontline action in the war.

Grandfather Osborne, from Allen's mother's side, still lived in the village at Cypress House and must have sold some cattle. The horse sale at Evercreech Junction near where they used to farm at Peking Mill would no doubt have been well attended with buyers. Competition would have been fierce. As recorded earlier, half a million horses – around half of all those working on farms – had been sent to work in the army.

21. A Letter to Elsie

Tuesday night 17th September

Dear Elsie,

I am sending back my box again so as you can send it back full again. I expect it shall be the last time I shall want it. They say we shall be on leave about next Friday week. I do not know for sure if it is right. I will let you know next week for sure. I suppose you have finished harvest by now, the weather seems to be very unsettled. I went out and seen Harold Weedon last Saturday but came back the same night because I forgot to get a pass, so I am going there for the weekend next Saturday. Is it right that Minnie Creighton has got a son. I suppose they are quite proud. I have not heard from you for the last few days, I hope you are all quite well as it leaves me the same. I have not much news to tell you this time.

With love,
From Allen

So it sounds like harvesting at home was probably done by now. Fortunately the wheat harvest across Britain in 1918 was good, which helped to alleviate the ongoing food crisis. Rationing on butter and sugar was to continue, however, until 1920 as the effects of war on trade and food production took time to heal. Over the course of the war, German U-boats sank two hundred and thirty ships bringing supplies to Britain.

22. A Letter Home

Friday night 20th September

I received the parcels quite safe today Saturday, the apple was quite a treat and must thank you very much for it. Will you send on the Journal this week. I am not going to Harold this week as I have to answer the phone Saturday night, it is a fresh order come out that we have to take it in turns. Tell Elsie that I shall not be able to give him my love for her. I suppose there were a good lot of people to the Red Cross. I am glad to hear that Mr Allen is getting on. I hope next week this time that I shall be home. They say we shall have our leave about next Saturday. I had a post-card from Nelson Naish and he said he should be home about the same time, so I shall be able to see him. I hope you are all quite well as it leaves me the same.

With love to all from Allen

An article in the *Shepton Mallet Journal* of 20th September 1918 reported on a British Farmers' Red Cross Day on the Townsend Field in Shepton Mallet where the Tesco retail park now stands. Livestock and produce were brought into a tented market place to be auctioned off to raise funds for the Red Cross overseas work.

'Three tents had been erected, one filled with a complexity of goods ... They comprised goats, a lamb, poultry, a goose, rabbits (live and dead), potatoes, marrows, parsnips, beet, grapes, peaches, cheese, groceries ... The second tent was very busily occupied later in the afternoon, dispensing refreshments of light kind, daintily served. The third canvas afforded shelter for the officials ... At a stand erected in another part of the field the Australian Band of about thirty members, in khaki, discoursed good music afternoon and evening, to the delight of large crowds.'

Lady Muriel Paget from Paget Hall in Cranmore made a speech regarding conditions in Russia and Eastern Europe where she had been travelling. Paget Hall would in later years become All Hallows' School which my own children would later attend. The article states:

'Her Ladyship gave some particulars of her visit to the south of Russia, and of her experiences at Lutsk and other centres, when she encountered 600,000 wounded in a week, and no surgeons:- where the wounded lay unattended on the ground in a plague of flies ... They had two raids a day on their hospital: and on one occasion when they were so full that thousands of men lay in the yards, they saw aeroplanes coming over the horizon like mosquitos ... In one instance an aeroplane had to come down and the airmen kept off the Russians by machine guns. Eventually a cow charged the machine and broke the propeller.'

23. A Letter Home

Wednesday night 25ᵗʰ Sept 1918

Dear Mother,

I am sending back my boxes and salt bag tonight. I do expect I shall be home on leave about Friday, if I am not back by Friday dinner time, I shall not be back before Saturday. The railway men have come out on strike and I think it has delayed us a day because there are no trains running down here. I suppose you have heard about it. I shall bring back my cycle with me and then I shall be able to ride it from Castle Cary station. I hope you are all quite well as it leaves me the same.

With love from Allen

Railway workers had become unhappy that other workers in munitions factories and even some in temporary jobs earned more than them despite their long years of experience in the job. The railways were privately owned but had been taken under government control during the war. Despite an offer from government being accepted by union leaders, the railway workers voted to come out on strike.

24. A Letter Home on a Re-used Scrap of Paper

Dear Mother,

I am sending back my watch as I cannot get it to go. So I shall have to do without one. We are going tonight with the 7 o'clock train from Weymouth. So do not write before you hear from me again. I hope you are all quite well as it leaves me the same in the pink, so do not worry.

With love to you all from Allen

25. A Letter to Allen

Banks Farm,
Chesterblade,

Thursday afternoon

Dr Allen,

I had your letter this morning pleased to hear that you are well. We have been busy using the drill it does its work very well put the wheat in Big Mead and the beans in Little Paddock. D put in Mrs Treasures wheat today. Mr Allen is getting on better. I am glad to tell you Mr Crees and H. Brock (hole in letter) today and looking at Mr Allen's pigs. Ours are gone and we sell the milk. Mr Allen's milk went today for the first time. I am glad to hear you saw Naish and Sealy, you must tell us more news next time you write. I am glad to see the war is getting so much better. Elsie had a letter from B. White he is not gone from his camp yet. Jim has a weeks holiday. We had 6 shillings 2 pence for eggs this week.

We are all well and pleased to hear you are the same. Aunt P. is about the same. With love from us all,

Mother
PS Had your watch quite safe.

26. A Letter Home

Friday night 4ᵗʰ Oct

Dear Mother,

I got sent back to camp about 11 o'clock. There were only 25 or 26 of us came back out of 70. There are 9 black soldiers here they come from South America you never seen such ugly devils as they are they make us laugh to see them drill sometimes they will only do what they like. The Bloody old Serg Major has got something to shout about now. Cary has not come back yet, but I expect him tonight. They say we shall be going to France next Tuesday. I heard that young Pole and Claycee went last Wednesday, I do not know if it is right. I went back with Tiny. I am going to try and enjoy myself the next few days I am in Weymouth. I will send you a PC when I leave Weymouth.

Hope you are all quite well as it leaves me the same,
fit as a fiddle with love to you all
from Allen
Ask Jim how his trousers are Old piss trousers.

This may well have been one of Allen's first encounters with people with a different skin colour to his own. There were no South Americans serving at this time so the soldiers he alludes to in his letter are most likely some of the sixteen thousand West Indian or seventy-four thousand South African soldiers who fought in the British Army during the Great War.

Departure to France and into the war was only a few days away now.

27. A Letter to Elsie

7th October 1918
Monday night

Dear Elsie,

I have had the watch tonight and I could not get it to go. I am sending back a stick of soap for Dad. I hope you are all quite well as it leaves me the same. They say we shall be going to France Wednesday. I do not know whether it is correct or not. Have not much news to tell you this time.

With love from Allen
How is Jim and his trousers ask him about 'Some mora'

The brotherly ribbing of my grandfather continues over his trousers and whatever that may have been and there's some sort of in-joke about 'some mora'!

28. A Postcard from a Friend

Dear Allen,

In answer to your PC I was rather surprised to hear you are off so soon. I hope this will reach you before you go. I went up with the milk this morning and saw Eileen she came up for a parcel and we went over to the milk factory. I only had two hours to wait before I could empty my milk, then I said 'some Mora'. Last Tues was rather a failure not many turned up. Bert went off last Thursday and woke up and found himself in camp Friday Morning and of course he said 'some Mora' civil words.

Yours sincerely,

Doris

The 'some mora' in-joke continues between friends!

29. A Postcard to Allen

Dr Allen,

Had your letter this am & parcel. Glad to hear you are quite well. Hope your watch will go alright & keeps good time. Jim is very well and all the rest, write again when you can.

With love from all, Mother

This is the last letter or postcard that was sent or received on home soil between Allen and his family and friends before he left for France.

PART FOUR
FRANCE

1. Leaving England

As well as the letters and postcards, the old bag in the attic also contained an old, brown leather diary in which Allen outlined the places he went in the army after leaving the training camp at Wyke Regis. In February 2018, one hundred years after he undertook this journey, I decided to retrace the same journey to try to understand what this experience would have been like for him.

On the first page of the diary, the following is written in Allen's handwriting:

42915 3rd Dorsets
D.I.B.D.
B.E.F. France
SM Britts
Col Welden
General Bazell

B.E.F. relates to the British Expeditionary Force in France and presumably the names below it are various people in the army that were to be of significance to Allen.

On the second page, Allen had written out a timeline of events detailing his movements once he left the training camp at Wyke Regis. The first two lines read:

10.10.18 Left Weymouth for Folkestone at 5pm arrived at 5am.

11.10.18 Left Folkestone 10am arrived Boulogne 2pm.

Allen's two hundred mile journey from Weymouth to Folkestone took twelve hours, travelling all through the night, and I can only imagine what all the young men must have been feeling during this journey as they made their way towards the war after a few cursory weeks of training. During Edwardian times, Folkestone had become a fashionable coastal town, but during the war it became an important transit port. Around 9.7 million troops passed through the harbour during the war, either leaving to fight in France or further afield, or returning home on leave or injured. Troop trains serviced the harbour and this was almost certainly how Allen arrived here. Eight hundred and fifty thousand Red Cross workers also travelled through the port, in both directions, during the war.

Folkestone had become extremely multinational, with the Chinese Labour Corps and Canadian soldier bases located in the town, while the hospitals were full of injured men from a multitude of different origins. Forty thousand Canadian troops were based in barracks in the town. Around ninety-six thousand Chinese workers either lived in and around Folkestone or passed through the town on their way to the front. The British began recruiting Chinese people through 1917-18 to replenish workers in munitions factories and ports and other tasks. Their contribution, however, was airbrushed from history until more recent times.

Thousands of Belgian refugees had arrived in September 1914 following the German invasion of their country and they were assisted by the town and dispersed around Folkestone and further afield. Around one hundred and twenty thousand refugees would arrive in Folkestone during the course of the war. A Belgian Relief Fund in the town provided six thousand free meals for refugees every day. Fifty refugees also travelled to Frome by train.

A troop train in Folkestone Harbour with troops waiting for a ship in the harbour quay

German Zeppelin attacks from the air had caused much damage to the town. Zeppelins were rigid air ships named after the man who pioneered them, Count Ferdinand von Zeppelin. The worst air raid in Folkestone was on 25 May 1917. In Tontine Street alone, one device left seventy-one people dead and injured at least ninety-four. Over the course of the war, Zeppelins killed over five hundred people across Britain during bombing raids.

The Mole Café, a free canteen offering tea, cake and buns to soldiers, sailors and Red Cross workers passing through, was set up in 1915 in the harbour area. Local volunteers staffed the café, and two of these helpers, sisters Margaret and Florence Jeffery, were awarded the Order of the British Empire, the Queen Elizabeth Medal (Belgium) and the Medal of Gratitude (France) for their services. There is something quintessentially English about two tea ladies being showered with war medals for keeping the refreshments flowing in a crisis! The two sisters started a visitor book for their transient customers to sign and between 1915 and 1919 some forty-three and a half thousand people signed the visitor book. These were subsequently bound into eight volumes of three and a half thousand pages and in 2014 were archived by Kent County Council to be used as a free resource for children to trace their relatives and in memory of those who never returned home again. Famous guests at the café included Winston Churchill (First Lord of the Admiralty at the time), David Lloyd George and Arthur Conan Doyle, and their signatures can be found in the visitor book.

After arriving at 5am following a twelve hour journey from Weymouth, Allen is quite likely to have called into the Mole Cafe for refreshments before his ship sailed at 10am. I wonder if Margaret or Florence served him that day? From Folkestone, the ominous sound of the guns in France and Belgium could be heard which must have been a surreal sound to hear for the first time. The first-hand reality of war was now not far away for the soldiers.

The Mole Café during the war with the visitor book under the flags

My pilgrimage to retrace Allen's journey to France began at 5am one February morning in 2018. After travelling by train from Frome, I arrived at Paddington and transferred across to St. Pancras. From here, I sped my way down towards the sea and my rendezvous with my great uncle in Folkestone; the place from where he would have waved goodbye to England, not knowing if he would ever return to her shores again.

As the train slowed to a stop at Folkestone Central, the other passengers in the carriage disembarked and I walked out into the town. I have to admit I felt quite emotional about this trip. I had spent months researching anything and everything in connection with Allen's story and it had become all-consuming. On the way down to the harbour area where Allen would have first arrived by train, I stopped off at the museum where I knew there was currently an exhibition regarding the Chinese Labour Corps who were posted in the town during the war. I explained my pilgrimage to a museum official in the reception area and she told me about the other memorials to the war in the town that would be worth a visit. The museum doesn't contain a great deal about the war but the story of the Chinese Labour Corps is a fascinating one that bears retelling.

At the outbreak of war, China was transitioning from Empire to Republic and aligning itself with the cause of the Allies was seen as a way of putting itself onto the world stage. It would also be a way of stemming the influence of Japan in the region and recovering lost possessions from the Germans in Shandong Province. Britain increasingly needed to resupply its army with more men that were employed in factory work at home. With an influx of Chinese workers, more British men could be channelled into the army and this problem would be solved. In early 1917, therefore, Chinese workers were recruited from the northern territory of Weihaiwei, where poverty and the allure of higher wages ensured a plentiful supply of men. Applicants had to be in good health and between the ages of twenty and forty.

The journey to Europe from China by sea and over land across North America was a long and arduous one, as the seas were rough and the danger from German U-boat attack in the Atlantic Ocean was a constant risk. Around seven hundred would die during this journey. On arrival in Europe, they were distributed to different locations, where they undertook various tasks in munition engineering. At ports and railway stations, they helped build and maintain frontline and road infrastructures. In Folkestone, a camp of two thousand Chinese men was established. Further batches of men, three thousand at a time, would arrive and then be sent onwards to France to work.

After the war, the Chinese were instrumental in reinstating French farmland back into food production by clearing landmines and installing drainage ditches to help feed the hungry populations of France and Belgium. They were also involved in mass reburials of dead soldiers. Although not serving as soldiers on the frontline, around three thousand Chinese lost their lives helping the Allies. Causes of death came from being targeted by German attack as well as accidents in the dangerous work they undertook. The influenza epidemic was, however, the biggest killer.

After the war, most of the Chinese workers returned home, although a significant number did stay and settled in France. China did not, however, end up recovering its lost possessions from Germany in Shandong Province, as these instead went to Japan. This incensed China and they refused to sign the Treaty of Versailles because of it.

After looking at the amazing photos in the Chinese Labour Corps exhibition in Folkestone, I headed up to the cliff top commemorative promenade. Down below, a yellow shingle beach stretched along the shore. A handful of walkers strolled along a wooden walkway that snaked across the pebbles. At the end of the promenade, on the cliff top, a memorial statue came into view. It was sited in the middle of a roundabout and large poppy wreaths had been laid at its base. To its right, stood a silver-coloured Centenary Arch. This had been erected in 2014 to mark the centenary of the start of the war and had been opened by Prince Harry.

Underneath the arch a circular inscription on the floor marked all the different peoples from around the world that passed through Folkestone during the war; spoken-word tributes to the fallen played out from hidden speakers. A series of plaques paid tribute to the many and varied stories of people passing through here, from Belgian refugees to nurses, and from Canadian troops to the local inhabitants who died in air raids. Black metal railings adorned with thousands of handmade woollen poppies ran along the length of the clifftop next to the promenade. This trail of woven flowers continued along the railings down Remembrance Road and down to the harbour area. A plaque at the top of the road read:

1914 1918

ROAD

OF

REMEMBRANCE

During the Great War tens of thousands of
British Soldiers passed along this road on their way
to and from the battlefields of Europe
'AT THE GOING DOWN OF THE SUN,
AND IN THE MORNING WE WILL REMEMBER THEM.'

Remembrance Road, Folkestone

Halfway down the road, lines from a poem by Carol Ann Duffy written in response to a Wilfred Owen poem, were carved onto tablets of sandy coloured stone fixed to the side of the cliff face. It read:

DOWN THE QUIET ROAD, AWAY, AWAY, TOWARDS
THE DYING TIME,
LOVE WENT, BRAVE SOLDIER, THE SONG DWINDLING;
WALKED TO THE EDGE OF ABSENCE; ALL MOMENTS GOING,
GONE; BELLS THROUGH RAIN
TO FALL ON THE CARVED NAMES OF THE LOST.

At the bottom of Remembrance Road, a dozen small boats bobbed in a penned-off quay and old, low brick archways marked the entrance to the fish market area. Uneven cobblestones paved the roads and past generations of fishing communities were still in evidence in the shop names. Jutting out into the English Channel was the Harbour Arm, a manmade concrete and stone jetty that cradled the harbour area from the open sea. I climbed the steps to the top of the fish market archways until the old disused railway tracks that brought Allen's troop train to the harbour quay were visible. I had already seen photos of this area on the internet but the area had clearly been regenerated since they were taken. The overgrown and rusty facades of these photos had now been replaced with fresh paint, flower beds grew between the old rail tracks and new walkways had been laid along the sides.

Railway platforms where Allen's troop train disembarked in Folkestone

I walked along the tracks over a bridge that linked the mainland to the Harbour Arm and spied ahead two workmen labouring behind mesh fencing on the next phase of the redevelopment. Behind them, the old station platforms curved away out of sight on either side of the pair of rail tracks where the troops disembarked during the war. They told me this phase of the development would be opening in time for Easter. The station buildings would be occupied by shops, restaurants and cafes, and a series of events and entertainments would be taking place. Despite being closed off to the public, I persuaded them to let me in behind the fence to take some photos once I had told them about my pilgrimage.

The Mole Cafe next to the harbour troop train tracks as it is today

I continued along the Harbour Arm as the tracks carried on, further out into the sea. The tracks bent round to pull up alongside a docking area where the troops had boarded the ships that carried them to France. A familiar set of buildings came into view at the harbour side: the site of the Mole Café where the two sisters served the troops a hundred years ago. The rusty old buildings had been rejuvenated with fresh paint and the old café had now reopened in the summer for the tourists. I had mixed feelings about this. On the one hand, it's amazing to think that, one hundred years on from when this place had hustled and bustled with troops, nurses, refugees and Chinese workers, it was being reinstated as a museum piece to their memory. On the other hand, for me, its becoming a tourist attraction detracted from the momentous things that were happening back then. I found it to be too much of an amusement park and not enough a place of reflection, but time will tell how it will be viewed in the future.

The atmosphere among the nineteenth-century buildings of Folkestone was relaxed; much of the old town existed from yesteryear but it was trying to modernise. The shops on the steep, winding cobblestones of the Old High Street as I wandered back through the town to the railway station were arty and bohemian. Funded art projects were dotted around the town in surprising places; four colourful mini-statues sat on ledges under a rusting railway bridge and carried plaques with inspiring and positive messages. The long wall that funnelled into the railway station had an impressive one hundred bronze cast hands, each different and representing every year between 1900 and 2000. Instinctively I lingered on the hand for 1918.

I caught a train to Dover as boats no longer go across the Channel from Folkestone, which had been one of the busiest crossing points to war-torn France. On the railway platform a group of school children were being rounded up and hustled together by their sheepdog-like teachers. It was half term and I guessed they were on a school trip somewhere. I took a seat in the waiting room and charged up my phone from an electric socket. A man sat across the room from me, eating a pastry out of a paper bag and hunched over a newspaper crossword. He wore a university scarf and trench coat but I noticed the heels were worn down unevenly on his scuffed shoes. He was in his mid-fifties and the glasses he wore around his greying temples gave him the air of an intellectual. Every few minutes he discreetly pulled a mini-bar bottle of whiskey from his coat pocket and poured a little into his bottle of coke on the table. His face was ruddy, suggesting this might be the habit of years. It was mid-afternoon.

I caught my train, arrived in Dover and hailed a taxi to transfer down to the ferry docks, sharing a cab with a French lady on her way home to Boulogne. We were two of only seven walk-on passengers for the crossing to Calais along with a mixture of drive-on cars and lorries. Today's trade of goods back and forth with Europe is in immense contrast to the troops, nurses, refugees and munitions that were doing this journey a hundred years ago. Calais has become infamous in recent years for its makeshift refugee camps. How differently we treat refugees today. In 1914, thousands of refugees, like the Belgians who fled their homes, were welcomed, housed, fed and cared for and had the sympathy of the British authorities and population. Today, the displaced peoples seeking refuge from war and authoritarian rule are viewed with contempt by many and are no longer universally welcomed. Our relationship with Europe is once again strained, but now in an altogether different way, born of pro-Brexit isolationism.

Our ferry, the Pride of Burgundy, eventually left port. I looked back at the disappearing land and tried to imagine what it would have felt like for Allen, packed on a troop ship with thousands of others. After a five hour wait in Folkestone, he and his fellow soldiers set sail at 10am on 11th October 1918 for a four hour crossing to Boulogne, arriving at 2pm. For many, this would have been the first time they had left their country of birth and emotions must have been high as they saw the white cliffs of Dover disappear from view. For many, this would also be the last time they would see home soil.

Leaving the white cliffs of England on the Pride of Burgundy

2. Boulogne to Rouen

Boulogne has long had a historic importance to Britain. In Roman times, the city was the Romans' main port for trade and communication with Britain. Following the collapse of the Roman Empire, a Germanic occupation was superseded by the Kingdom of France during the Middle Ages, and the city was even occupied by the Kingdom of England on numerous occasions whilst the two powers battled each other. Napoleon used Boulogne as a staging area in 1805 during his planned invasion of Britain. The city's twelfth century belfry is a UNESCO World Heritage Site and its fishing port is the largest in France.

Right from the beginning of the Great War, Boulogne, along with Calais and Dunkirk, were to be important ports for the British Expeditionary Force, and there would be a large military presence in the region throughout the war. The proximity of this length of Northern French coast, known as the Opal Coast, made it an ideal landing zone for establishing troops in France. Around 1.7 million troops passed through Boulogne during the war and the area hosted numerous camps and military organisations. Around one thousand three hundred officers and seventy thousand troops were based in the town and almost half of all the imports required to service the war effort in France during the latter part of the war came through the three ports here.

A temporary hospital in Boulogne during the war

Some of the largest hospitals were set up in Boulogne and nearby Wimereux and Etaples, treating the wounded and caring for those that were too injured to travel. In Etaples alone, twenty hospitals provided twenty thousand beds for the wounded. Depots were also established in the region to store munitions, weapons and food, with road and rail used for transport back and forth to the front line. Up until 1918, the Germans had not attacked this region much, but this changed as the war ground on and German air raids on depots and transport infrastructure began under the cover of darkness.

Arriving here on a packed troop ship at 2pm after a four hour journey by sea on 11 October 1918, Boulogne was Allen's first taste of a foreign land and must have seemed a veritable hive of activity. Docking in Calais after my own journey across the Channel, I once more shared a taxi, this time to Boulogne Railway Station, with my French companion. On arrival,

I booked into a hotel near the docks where Allen would have disembarked and headed off to bed after a meal in the hotel restaurant. I was awoken at 5am by French youths in the street shouting, revving cars and messing about. They had been out all night at clubs; it had been a Friday night. I watched them for a while out my window and wondered if they appreciated that a hundred years ago they would have been the ones sent off to fight in the trenches.

HMTS Victoria was a troop ship used for carrying troops from
Folkestone to Boulogne during the Great War

I couldn't get back to sleep so I rose early and walked down to the harbour where Allen's ship had docked. It was quiet this early on a Saturday morning except for the early bustle of fishermen getting their fish market stalls ready along the old cobblestone quayside. As I wandered down through the harbour towards the sea, I passed a large metal sculpture called 'Shake Hands' in commemoration of the Entente Cordiale between France and Britain. It was a reminder of how we still have more in common with our European neighbours than separates us, and how we would still come to each other's aid should we be in need. The Great War years were a truly extraordinary time and the sacrifices made to help people in other countries were enormous and this sculpture somehow recognises that. As the harbour water opened out into the sea, an area of beach stretched out to the right and I imagined Allen's ship coming into port from across the waves.

Boulogne harbour where Allen's troop ship from Folkestone docked

'Shake Hands' sculpture in Boulogne harbour

That day, all there was to see was a lone fishing boat quietly chugging back into the harbour with a hungry flock of seagulls in enthusiastic pursuit, in the hope of some cast-off fish. The small boat docked alongside the fish market and started to unload its catch. Customers bustled around, hovering over the rich colours and smells of the many different sea foods on offer overlooked by two colourful statues, Batisse and Zabelle. A plaque explained these were two characters of local folklore: Batisse the fisherman represented Boulogne's enduring fishing trade as did Zabelle, his wife, dressed in traditional attire alongside him.

I passed another Saturday morning market, this time a mixture of fruit, vegetables, meats and pastries, as I made my way up the hill along more cobbled streets to the impressive city walls of the Old Town. The cathedral and majestic buildings within the ancient walls dated back to the time of counts reigning over their estates; recent excavations had found Roman remains. Beneath the cathedral were France's largest crypts. These were a complex myriad of catacombs, passageways and rooms, all covered in what could best be described as ancient graffiti. Their excavation had only been recent but I wondered if Allen came up to the Old Town during his brief time in Boulogne. He would at least have seen it looking down over the city from up on the hill. The city now had the feel of a modest fishing port quietly getting on with its age old tradition.

The city walls of Boulogne's Old Town

The next entries in Allen's diary read:

12.10.18 Left Boulogne for Rouen 12am and arrived 4am Sunday morning

13.10.18 Kit inspection same day

14.10.18 Passed Gas Chamber

15.10.18 Fatigues

16.10.18 Ditto

The one hundred and fifteen mile trip south, near to the coast through Normandy from Boulogne to Rouen, only took Allen four hours so would have most likely been aboard one of the troop trains. To follow Allen there, I hired a car and hit the road. I decided to opt for the more relaxed scenic route rather than the motorway, and once out of the city, the scene outside the window quickly turned into the wide open spaces of arable farming with a noticeable lack of hedges and animals, very unlike the landscape back home in Somerset. It dawned on me that the reason the French eat so much bread and pastries is because of their huge expanses of crop land, predominantly wheat.

Single avenues of trees often bordered the road on either side. The flat, open land was occasionally punctuated with small villages and towns, or 'communes' as the French call them. I passed through Nouvion and my favourite place name, Huppy, then stopped for a break in Abbeville and went into a run-down looking *tabac*. Using my terrible GCSE French, I ordered coffee and bottles of water. The haggard-looking host and three henchmen at the bar spoke together in a drawled conversation as they watched some sort of horse and cart racing on the large screen on the wall. This wasn't a tourist town or place where visitors were catered for; I was very much out of place. Before I left, I used the WC, which was decorated in lurid bright green paint with strange plastic ivy snaking around the pipes from the toilet. Offering an ignored '*au revoir*' to my hosts, I headed for Rouen via Neufchatel-en-Bray.

Arriving at 4am on 13 October 1918, Allen would have found the ancient port city of Rouen on the Seine a busy place. Tucked away from the front line, it was a major logistics hub throughout the war with fifteen hospital bases accommodating twenty thousand beds across the city and on the outskirts. Apart from the obvious wounds and injuries that were occurring from the new horrors of mechanical warfare, there were also other less obvious problems to deal with. One British hospital treated wounded Prisoners Of War and British prisoners with self-inflicted wounds. Some other patients had problems which were not directly from the battlefield. A 'client for Rouen' became army slang for a patient with venereal disease. In the first year of the war alone, one hundred and seventy-one thousand men visited a brothel that had been established in the town and two hundred and forty-three cases of infection were reported. Public opinion back home in Britain was outraged and the brothel was forced to close.

Numerous burial grounds and cemeteries were established in the area and two Commonwealth War Grave Cemeteries were created on the outskirts of Rouen where burials from the hospitals took place. As well as being one of the main hospital bases for the BEF, Rouen had also become the main route of evacuation for casualties by railway, by ambulance, by barge down the Somme, and by char-à-bancs, which were horse drawn vehicles or early motor vehicles at this time.

Famous landmarks in Rouen include its Notre Dame cathedral, with its gothic façade, completed in the sixteenth century, the subject of a series of Monet paintings. The cathedral's Tour de Beurre, or butter tower, was financed by selling indulgencies for the consumption of butter during Lent. The graves of Henry the Young King and Richard the Lionheart, who were sons of King Henry II, can be found inside the cathedral. Rouen also has a famous castle where Joan of Arc was thought to have been brought in 1431 to be threatened with torture. The city is noted as well for its half-timbered buildings which have survived the ages.

Allen spent the next four days of his journey in Rouen and from his minimal diary entry of his time there, we know he underwent a kit inspection and had two days of 'fatigues' which would have involved getting kitted up with battlefield and camouflage dress from one of the many depots based in Rouen. Uniforms at this time were made of thick, woollen tunic dyed khaki topped with a stiffened peak cap. Around the ankles and calves, 'puttees', from the Hindi word *patti*, were worn in the form of wrapped around bandaged material. Footwear consisted of ammunition boots with hobnail soles. A narrow leather belt carried a water bottle, cartridge pouches and entrenching tool. A large haversack unpopular with troops completed the ensemble. The British were the only army to use camouflage at the beginning of the war, so there may have been some camouflage materials given out as well. Allen would also have been issued with a fixed bayonet rifle and gas mask.

Allen also noted he 'passed gas chamber', so this probably related to checking his gas attack equipment in a testing chamber. Poison gas was first used by the Germans at Ypres against Canadian and French troops on 22 April 1915. In response, troops were initially equipped with ineffectual cotton mouth pads for protection against further attack. This was then superseded by the Black Veil Respirator, which had chemical soaked mouth pads tied into place by a long cloth, but left the eyes exposed. The next development was the British Hypo Helmet in June 1915 made of a chemical absorbing fabric that covered the entire head, including the eyes. In reality it was an uncomfortable greasy, grey-felt bag with eye goggles that misted up and there was no way of expelling the build-up of carbon dioxide from the head bag. Allen would have been issued with the PH helmet canister gas mask which emerged after several development phases in 1916. These masks were connected by an outlet valve and hose to a tin can that contained carbon dioxide absorbent material inside to prevent build-up inside the mask. The use of gas during the war was a new development and its use was often not successful. There are accounts of how Allied use of gas would sometimes blow back into their own trenches and gas their own troops if the wind had not been taken account of accurately.

My first destination was the old part of town, where I wanted to find somewhere to park and a place to stay for the night. After circling the streets quite a few times I eventually found an underground car park beneath the impressive Palais de Justice.

In contrast to the quiet streets of Boulogne, the maze of old streets around Rouen was full of life and energy. Sunshine had brought a holiday atmosphere to the hordes of people that thronged the eateries and shops. The buildings were an amazing mix of huge gothic majesty and old timber framed antiquity and it felt like stepping back in time. This would have been the same at the time of Allen's visit here and Rouen's distance behind the front lines during two world wars had protected its architectural character. The Cathedral Notre Dame and a whole host of other churches and administrative buildings boasted impressive Gothic architecture. Among the old timber-framed buildings, however, there was a bohemian feel and it was here I found the quirky and arty *Hotel du Thé* to stay for the night. The hotel specialised in serving only tea and homemade cake and my funky loft bedroom overlooked the courtyard.

Cathedral Notre Dame, Rouen

Old timber-framed buildings, Rouen

In front of the more modern Hôtel de Ville, an impressive statue of Napoleon on horseback celebrated the Republic, although the pigeon which sat disrespectfully on his head took away much of his authority. One of the shops specialised in a surreal theme of British pop art alongside Monty Python, British post boxes and traffic lights. There was also an oversized red rabbit, a rocking horse hung upside down from the ceiling, and a skeleton jammed in amongst the menagerie of other items for sale. Everywhere, art galleries and shops were interspersed amongst the normal array of shops and brilliant graffiti adorned various shop shutters when they were pulled down at closing-time. There was a fun and salubrious atmosphere at night as people thronged the streets to eat and enjoy the nightlife. The city's wartime reputation and infamy for brothels didn't seem too far removed and the throng of soldiers back then would have provided a willing customer base.

The next day was Sunday, and a more relaxed feel inhabited Rouen as I bade farewell to its streets. I drove to the top of a hill which overlooked the city and was famous for its panoramic views. The gothic spires rose up out of the wooden streets in the early morning sunshine and gave no hint of the life of its sleepy inhabitants below.

3. Eastwards to the Front

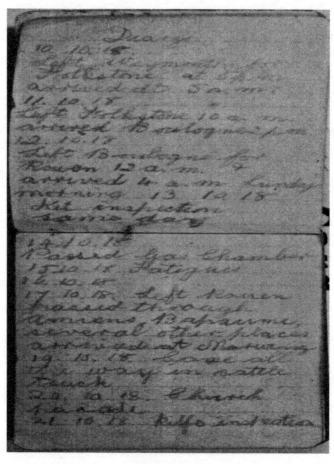

Pages in Allen's diary

After four days in Rouen getting kitted up, Allen moved on and wrote in his diary:

17.10.18 Left Rouen passed through Amiens, Bapaume, several other places arrived at Marcoing
19.10.18 Came all the way in a cattle truck
20.10.18 Church parade
21.10.18 Rifle inspection Left Marcoing

In the bag found in my cousin's attic, there was also a postcard dated 20 October 1918 sent by Allen from France.

Dear Mother,
Just a line to let you know that I am quite alright. I have finished my journey after 2 days in a cattle truck. I am about 20 miles from the firing line. I cannot tell you where I am or where I have been. I hope you are all quite well. So do not worry. Hope you have received my letter. With love to you all from Allen.

Another letter from the attic bag was written from Allen's mother.

Sunday morn Oct 20th 1918

My Dear Allen,

I had your letter and postcard this morning with your fresh address. I had your field card and other letter last Thursday and so I wrote back to you the same day. I hope you had it before you were moved on any further. We are glad to hear that you are quite well. I will tell you the news I put in the last letter in case you did not have it. Mr Crees and Mr Brock came up to see Mr Allen's (unreadable) and went out shooting, they shot 3 rabbits and 6 birds. I am pleased to tell you that Mr A is getting on nicely now he can walk about in the (unreadable) Mr Higgins the cheese dealer at Mr Carys is in the same (hole in paper) as Mr Allen so he has company now. Dad drilled Big Mead with the wheat and the drill does its work very well and the little paddock into beans and drilled Mrs Treasures wheat, Mr Allen broad casted his instead using the drill, the pigs are sold & the milk is going the last fortnight. Mabel is leaving and her sister I expect will take her place. A. James's wife has a baby son last week. Your aunts and Grandma and Granf about the same, Elsie is going down to stay with your Aunt Pat at Evercreech Mrs Pitney is going away for a week, Elsie has the flags to sell for our day next Thursday. Annie Giles is dead that lived at Batcombe with Jim James, she was taken into the hospital and passed away the same day. I had 6/2 for eggs last week. I have put you in a list of the following sales I thought you would like to see them. I hear that Winnie Nelson is trying to take the farm at Doulting where E. Candy lives and he is going into Mr W. Candy's farm. Elsie had a letter from B. White he is not gone from his camp yet, that was last week, he wants your address sent to him, Elsie had a letter (hole in paper) to Alford and they can send it to him.

With love from all, hoping you are quite well.

Mother

Life back in Somerset at this time as relayed by Allen's mother was in such striking contrast to Allen's experiences moving through France as a soldier, on his way to fight at the front. The travel and bustle of wartime city life in places like Boulogne and Rouen would have been like nothing he had known before; a Somerset farm lad nineteen years of age thrust into the logistics of war. Riding in the back of a cattle truck the one hundred and thirty-five miles from Rouen to Marcoing, Allen passed through Amiens. The city is divided by the river Somme and is known for its Gothic cathedral and nearby medieval belfry, narrow streets, and floating market gardens on the city's canals, but had suffered greatly during the war.

During the German spring offensive on the Western Front in March 1918 following the Bolshevik uprising in Russia, the Germans attacked the vital railway junction at Amiens. The Allies rallied and the Battle of Amiens began on 8 August 1918. This was the opening phase of the Allied Hundred Days Offensive that was to lead ultimately to the end of the war. The Allies advanced over seven miles on the first day, which was one of the greatest advances of the entire war. This marked an end to the period of stagnant trench warfare as mobile armoured attacks became the new favoured form of offensive. Five hundred and eighty tanks were used during this attack, and the effect of this led to a large surrender of German troops as their personnel and supplies reached exhaustion. Their defeat gave a boost in morale to the Allied war effort.

A woman travelling with a cow in Amiens March 1918

On leaving Rouen, I followed Allen's route to Amiens in my hire car, which was luxury compared to his ride in the back of a cattle truck squashed in with his fellow troops. I now travelled through the Somme region and the countryside en route was much the same as between Boulogne and Rouen: flat wide open arable farmland devoid of animals, trees and hedgerows. It was Sunday so the streets were quiet and on entering the city, road workers seemed to be digging up half of the city's road network. I had booked a hotel in the centre close to Amiens' Gothic Notre Dame Cathedral. What hit me straight away was the change in atmosphere in the place. Amiens suffered greatly in the Great War from German attacks, and unlike Rouen, the buildings were mostly newly built apart from a massive gothic cathedral rising up above it. The mainly red brick modern architecture felt rather soulless and quiet after the bustle of Rouen.

After checking into my hotel, I wandered past the cathedral. Its spires are the highest of any cathedral in France and I was surprised to find its doors locked. Only handfuls of people wandered through the streets and the air felt chilled after the sunshine of Rouen. The hotel suggested getting lunch across the river where half a dozen restaurants lined the Somme River and I took the last remaining table outside a restaurant called *L'Usine*.

After ordering a French beer and lunch, I looked around to take in the view and noticed a wooden sculpture of a man in the middle of the still waters of the river. He appeared to be gazing up at the impressive cathedral. It's only later I discovered by chance another wooden sculpture of a female companion high on a ledge on the end wall of a red brick house, to the left of the cathedral view from the riverbank; a clever piece of al fresco art that required a bit of work to make sense of it. Just along from my lunch table, a busking guitarist was ignored as he went through a repertoire of Pink Floyd, Bob Marley and Leonard Cohen. I discovered that the restaurant had forgotten my food order when I asked after forty minutes if it was going to take much longer, so they gave me a free beer and knocked up something quickly in the kitchen.

The view across the Somme towards Notre Dame Cathedral in Amiens

After lunch I followed the river along to the Hortillonnages, a serene and tranquil maze of canals and garden allotments, each with its own bridge crossing the water to a patch of garden and a small house. Each bridge had its own individual style complete with an odd looking door in the middle of it. It was picture postcard stuff and the river walkways were busy with Sunday strollers, cyclists and joggers. In the summer, the gardeners sell garden produce from boats on the river. Walking back into town, I took in the local sights of Jules Verne's house with its colourful courtyard façade that covered the entire end of a neighbouring house, and the Cirque, a permanent octagonal building where he established a circus in the early

1900s. The building was still used for occasional concerts. Elsewhere in town, an old belfry had survived the bombs but little else was of historical note apart from a few old wooden-framed buildings down by the river where university students lived. It all looked pretty run down.

Hortillonnages garden allotment area of Amiens

Around the town, a variety of large posters were pasted onto walls in commemoration of 'La Grande Guerre', each with a twitter hashtag of '*#amiens*' written in the corner and the phrase '*Among us*'. Most of the posters looked old and faded and I wondered if they were from commemorations in 2014 to mark the beginning of the war. The largest and only new looking of these was a banner along the entrance to the railway station. Local skateboarders rattled backwards and forwards along the station's long, sloping entrance walkway. Later that night, students came out onto the streets to drink in the bars along the river but the overall air of Amiens was still much more tranquil than Rouen. It felt a little lost and lacking in soul and I wondered if this was a hangover from the destruction of its historical heart during the war.

Leaving Amiens early the next morning, I walked down the stairway of the underground car park and noticed a strong smell of menthol, presumably to combat the usual smell of urine that most car park stairwells emit. The car park had only cost one euro for about twenty hours of parking and went straight on my top three car parks of all-time list. The Monday morning drive out of Amiens, through the industrial eastern side of the city, was much busier with traffic than the casual Sunday drivers from the day before. My route out negotiated around yet more traffic lights through the industrial eastern side of the city and with just as many roadworks.

A commemorative banner at Amiens railway station

After Amiens, Allen next travelled thirty miles to Bapaume in the back of a cattle truck, so I headed east along the road he would have taken. The countryside differed here from the landscape around Boulogne and Rouen. I was now in the heart of the Somme region. The fields of crops had darker, richer looking soils, and were larger in size and farmed more intensively. The towns and villages lost the quaint nature they held in the days before and were characterised by industrial units and factories. Bypassing the towns of Albert and Ovillers, signs started to appear by the roadside demarking the location of the frontline in 1916. The atmosphere of everything felt darker and the weather had turned cold and grey in contrast to the bright winter sunshine of the previous days.

The Somme region

I drove on another mile and was stopped in my tracks by the sudden appearance by the roadside of a huge stone monument surrounded by walls that extended away into the misty landscape and covered an area of about an acre. In the middle of the bleak landscape it stood out like an alien form. I was struck by a feeling of 'Oh my God, this actually happened'. Until I saw it first-hand, the horrors of the war had just been words on a page in a history book. Now it was there in front of my face and under my feet. I parked on the side of the road and got out of my car. It was bitterly cold and a sharp wind cut across the bare landscape. The entrance to the cemetery was a large pale stone archway with around a dozen Romanesque columns extending along to large stone corner pillars. From there, huge walls extended around the entire site with dozens of columns placed in front on them. As I approached the entrance, rows and rows of uniform pale gravestones could be seen through the roadside columns. It was shocking. Flowerbeds were neatly tended in rows at their base, and the grass was neatly shorn all around the site. Two workmen worked making repairs to a wall in the corner and a sign apologised for any inconvenience.

This was the Pozières British Cemetery and Memorial. A plaque told the story:

The village of Pozières and the surrounding farmland were fiercely contested during the Allied offensive on the Somme which began on 1 July 1916. Initially an objective for the first day, this ground was taken by Commonwealth forces three weeks later. Pozières British Cemetery is the final resting place of nearly 2,800 Commonwealth soldiers, most of whom fell in 1916. Nearly half of those buried here remain unidentified, but among them are more than 1,800 who served in regiments of the United Kingdom, more than 700 men of the Australian Imperial Force, and over 200 who fought with Canadian units.

Pozières British Cemetery and Memorial

Pozières was lost in March 1918 during the German Spring Offensive, and recaptured by the Allies in August. Around the cemetery stands the Pozières Memorial, which commemorates those who fought on the Somme in 1918. It bears the names of their fallen comrades who have no known grave, including more than 300 men of the forces of South Africa, and over 14,300 who served with British regiments, most of whom fell in March and April 1918.

On 21 March 1918, the Germans launched an offensive named Operation Michael against Allied forces around the Somme. By 25 March, this ground had been lost and the town of Albert soon followed. Nearly 8,000 men named on the Pozières Memorial were killed in the first four days of the offensive, when Commonwealth soldiers struggled to resist massed German forces, including specially equipped and trained assault units known as sturmtruppen. Within two weeks the Germans had advanced around 65 kilometres. They were eventually halted at Villers-Bretonneux by British and Australian troops on 4 and 5 April 1918. On 8 August, Allied victory in the Battle of Amiens began an advance which would recapture this area on 24 August, and would only cease with the Armistice which ended the fighting on the Western Front.

A large lump in my throat formed as I walked slowly down the steps onto the grass and along the rows of graves. Each headstone bore the soldier's regimental emblem, his name, rank, age and date of death and the symbol of his religion. The ages of the men on the gravestones were mostly eighteen, nineteen and twenty, and the gravestones of those too badly injured to identify read '*A SOLDIER OF THE GREAT WAR. KNOWN UNTO GOD*'. At the far end, a large stone cross with a bronze sword set against it looked down upon the gravestones and carved onto the large rectangle of stone it stood on were the words '*THEIR NAME LIVETH FOR EVERMORE*'. This phrase came from the Wisdom of Sirach and was proposed by the poet laurate, Rudyard Kipling, whose only son had been killed during the war.

On the three long walls that surrounded the cemetery were carved the names of the thousands who died in the Somme but who had no known grave. It was all very affecting and I began to ask myself how this was ever allowed to happen? How could human beings be so destructive and so stupid? Thousands of lives were lost fighting over a frontline that moved to and fro across a really small area of land. For four years! That this then happened again just over twenty years later is almost beyond belief. As I stood there, the futility and stupidity was truly bewildering. An idea formed in me then that newly elected politicians in Europe should have to visit the mass war graves on its lands as part of an induction process before being given the responsibilities of power.

I walked back through the gravestones to the entrance and stopped to sign a visitor book. There had been a constant stream of visitors there, mainly from the UK and Australia, some visiting relatives and some just paying their respects to the many. There was also a folder with a list of all those buried here and where in the cemetery you could find each individual grave if you were visiting someone in particular. I discovered that the light-coloured stone used for the headstones, walls and memorials was in fact Portland stone from the Isle of Portland adjacent to Wyke Regis where Allen's training camp back in England was based. An information page related how the War Graves Commission looked after the cemetery:

The care of this cemetery/memorial is the responsibility of the Commonwealth War Graves Commission. The Commission was established by Royal Charter during the First World War to mark and maintain the graves of the members of the forces of the Commonwealth who died in that war and to build and maintain memorials to the dead whose graves are unknown. Its duties were extended to include the dead of the Second World War and it is now responsible for commemorating 1,700,000 Commonwealth servicemen and women in about 145 countries around the world.

The cost of this work is shared by the Commonwealth countries that provided independent forces in the wars, who pay in proportions based on the numbers of their graves. Other Commonwealth countries contribute by maintaining graves in their own country.

The work is founded upon principles which have remained unaltered; that each of the dead should be commemorated individually by name either on the headstone on the grave or by an inscription on a memorial; that the headstones should be uniform; and that there should be no distinction made on account of military or civil rank, race or creed.

Pozières in 1918

As I walked back to my car, I stopped and looked back at the huge memorial set within this bleak February landscape. This was a sombre landscape with the weight of a terrible history hanging heavy on its shoulders. It was an exposed and cold place and winters in the trenches and mud here under the onslaught of war would have been truly awful. The air still felt heavy with death. When Allen passed through here on 17 October 1918 it would have been a scene of devastation.

A short distance on from the Pozières Memorial, another memorial appeared on the side of the road. This site was known as Windmill Hill: a memorial commemorating the deaths of nearly seven thousand Australian soldiers. They had lost their lives on that site between July and September 1916 battling to gain ground from the Germans on what was strategically important high ground. The modest memorial largely consisted of two flag poles and a plaque but as I walked around the site where the old windmill had stood, I was surprised to find another memorial in the field behind. It was makeshift in character in stark contrast to the imperial looking Pozières Memorial back down the road and a laminated piece of paper stuck to a bit of wood read:

The grassed area you see in front of you is the beginning of the Pozières Memorial Park which was inaugurated on 23 July 2016. The crosses depict 7000 Australian men who died in the Battle of Pozières liberating the village of Pozières in 1916. Of the 7000 men killed, 4112 were never found and have no grave. This is the first time in 100 years these men have ever been honoured with a cross where they rest. The crosses have been laid out in the design of the rising sun on the Australian Army slouch hat badge with the long axis of the design pointing towards Thiepval and Mouquet Farm. This Memorial Park has only been possible due to the kind donations by Australians to the Pozières Remembrance Association.

Out into the field, small wooden crosses around six inches high were inscribed with the words '*Australia 1916 Pozières*'. Each cross had a hand woven red poppy attached, and collectively they fanned out across the bleak landscape. Another memorial to all the animals that had died in the war had also been erected in recent times. A wooden sign read '*WW1 Animal War Memorial*' and a slightly strange and hackneyed U-shaped collection of animals on plinths sat alongside a small statue of St. Francis of Assisi, various plaques, a wagon wheel, park benches and tree plantings.

Crosses at the Australian Pozières Memorial Park

It appeared to have been a joint Australian and New Zealand venture and a plaque read:

'TO ALL THE ANIMALS
THEY HELD NO MALICE
THEY SERVED ALL NATIONS
THEY WORKED AND DIED
IN THE SERVICE OF MAN.'

The WW1 Animal War Memorial near Pozières

As I drove on, the green War Graves Commission signs denoting another cemetery of war dead became a familiar sight every few miles. The region was covered in cemeteries, some at the roadside, some out in the middle of a farmer's field, some large, some small. A flash of white on a hillside in the distance became a familiar sight as rows of white gravestones appeared like a white blanket. I passed through small towns and villages like Le Sars and Warlencourt, and eventually arrived at Bapaume which Allen mentioned in his diary.

Bapaume had been strategically important during the war due to its location as a junction where roads from all the directions of the compass met. Bapaume was occupied by the Germans on 26 September 1914 but had been taken back by the British on 17 March 1917. The Germans once again took the city on 24 March 1918 and so the Second Battle of Bapaume took place between 21 August and 3 September later that year, and formed part of the larger Allied One Hundred Day Offensive. Artillery bombardment and improved armoured support from tanks helped force holes through German trench lines. As the Allies eventually overran their opponents, the retreating German forces laid a trap consisting of a mine with a timer, and this exploded in the town hall just before Australian forces arrived. Bapaume had suffered greatly from these battles with most buildings left as rubble, including the church which was demolished by shelling in 1916.

I parked in the centre square next to the town hall and saw a plaque on the wall. It read:

The town of Bapaume built its first Town Hall and belfry, a symbol of the town's independence, during the twelfth century. The ground floor served as a merchants hall while the upper floor housed the council hall and a room which was used for public celebrations.

The current architecture of the Town Hall is similar to the previous, which was built between 1583 and 1611, but destroyed on 25 March 1917 after the explosion of a time bomb left behind by the Germans. After the slow and dangerous work of demining, it was rebuilt in its original location between 1931 and 1932.

A photo on the plaque shows the devastated town hall after it had been destroyed:

Bapaume Town Hall in 1917 after being destroyed by German forces

From Bapaume, Allen's cattle truck ride carried him another seventeen miles east to Marcoing, so I set off once more in that direction and passed a small war cemetery in a field of kale near Beaumetz-les-Cambrai, and another at a site called Delsaux Farm. I also visited a huge memorial at Louvenal that commemorates the horrendous losses suffered during the Battle of Cambrai in 1917. During twenty days of fighting, forty-four thousand British soldiers and fifty thousand German soldiers lost their lives. Their graves are spread among the numerous cemeteries near where they fell across the region. Seven thousand and forty-eight bodies were never found and the names of these men are inscribed and commemorated on the Louvenal Memorial. In the cemetery next to the memorial, the war dead include casualties from the Chinese Labour Corp who died clearing mines at the end of the war.

Louvenal Memorial

Beaumetz-les-Cambrai Military Cemetery No. 1

Eventually I arrived in the seemingly deserted village of Marcoing. There was not much of note here and I began to notice a pattern amongst all the places I passed through. Everything was newly built in predominantly red brick and all the places seemed to have the same 'Hôtel de Ville' town hall and church in identikit fashion. Each place had a memorial to their local war dead. Here, the memorial reads '*LA COMMUNE DE MARCOING A SES ENFANTS MORTS POR LA FRANCE*' and the names of the fallen are inscribed on the monument. Everything had been razed to the ground in this region as the frontline moved backwards and forwards across its land over a four year period. These places had all been rebuilt from scratch. This part of the Somme was characterised by small commune settlements and farmland and it felt half deserted. The lack of old historic buildings and new build architecture gave it a strange feel.

Marcoing became an important town during the Battle of Cambrai, when it was first captured by German forces on 20 November 1917. The town came under repeated Allied attack until it was evacuated by the Germans in early December 1917. It had been taken again by the Germans on 28 September 1918 but they were repelled once more shortly before Allen arrived here.

Marcoing during the war

After being billeted here for three days and undergoing a church parade and rifle inspection, Allen left on 21 October 1918. His next diary entry read:

21.10.18 arrived Walingcourt slept in old cottage.
22.10.18 left Walingcourt arrived at Inchy.

Many of the buildings in this battlefield area were destroyed and turned into piles of rubble. Surviving buildings would have been mostly deserted and the troops would have been able to shack up in some of these. Allen found an old cottage to sleep in after arriving at Walincourt-Selvigny, a small village around ten miles to the south east. I drove off along Allen's route and passed through Masnieres and over the canal at St. Quentin. En route, I passed by one of the few remaining old buildings, a beautiful large tithe barn building made of light coloured stone with large round towers on its corners. A little further on a large red brick abbey that dated back to 1255 had also survived the war and had been turned into a restaurant called *Abbaye des Guillemins*. Passing by those two old buildings made me think what a shame so much heritage had been destroyed by the war as the new buildings that took their place lacked soul. Centuries of history had been wiped from existence in four short years of insanity.

The landscape going east had changed from large wide open intensively farmed spaces to a more parochial, sleepy atmosphere with smaller fields and a slower pace of life. In contrast to the bleak landscape around Albert and Bapaume, it became harder to imagine a war zone in these smaller villages. Arriving in Walincourt-Selvigny, the small town took on the usual format of modern red brick houses, town hall and church.

From there, Allen had then travelled another eight miles further east to Inchy, and edged towards the front line. Inchy was a small village based around a large main road that ran between Cambrai and Le Cateau. A large red brick church sat at the top of the hill on the skyline.

It had been captured by the Allies on 3 October 1918 and the village became the site of a cemetery for fifty soldiers who all died in October 1918. Having travelled two hundred and sixty miles through France, Allen now joined up with the fighting force of A Company, 6th Dorsets, 50th Brigade, 17th Division, V Corps. Regimental diaries from this point on help add more detail to Allen's minimalist diary entries.

Inchy, 1918

The Regimental diaries described the weather as wet and dull, and the day was spent *'reorganising and having inspections'*. Machine guns had been captured in the town square. In anticipation of a renewed attack by the Allies, the forward areas had experienced heavy enemy shelling. The 17th Division, which Allen joined, had been relieved from the front line and had come back to Inchy to rest.

We know that Allen's 50th Brigade, whilst in reserve in Inchy, received operation orders at 10.30am on 23 October. They were to move forward in support of the attack by other Divisions. First, they were to parade at Inchy Cemetery, departing at 11.20am along Le Cateau Road to Amerval Ridge, marching in file along the road with Companies two hundred yards apart.

After almost three hours of marching, they arrived at Amerval Ridge at 2pm and stayed there until 6pm, after which time they left for billets in nearby Neuvilly.

One of the legacies of this time is how slang from the trenches began to enter the English language with words that are still in use today. Scraps of toilet paper that floated across the battlefield were nicknamed 'bum fodder' which became shortened to 'bumpf'. Being drunk started to be known as being 'blottoed', a 'dud' was something that didn't work, and 'lousy' and 'crummy' related to soldiers who were lice infested in the trenches.

Another letter in the attic bag for Allen from home, dated 25 October 1918 reads:

My Dear Allen,

We had your letter this morning that you wrote last Sunday and I wrote back the same day and the one the Thursday before, so you see I have written to you twice before this one. I should think you will have them by now. You write as often as you can and I will answer each even if it is only a few words so we can know you are alright as we are pleased to hear you were when you wrote. You don't tell us if you are with Cary now or not or any more that you knew at Wyke Regis we should like to know. I am glad to tell you Mr Allen came home last Monday he can drive about in the pony and trap. Elsie is down with your Aunt P. at Evercreech as she is very ill. I hope to go down tomorrow, you could write to her and ask her how she is. Dad is gone with the last bit of cheese today. Arthur M is gone to Bath today to be tested again. They finish pulling the mangolds today. Bob Hale has been home all the week with the flu. I must tell you Jim and the pony has been very busy the last ten days hauling the mangold leaves to the cows. Be sure and write when you can, it takes four days for us to have a letter. Aunt Elizabeth is gone to Ditcheat to stay for a few days. Mr and Mrs Crees have had the flu. Your Aunts and Granm and Granfather are very well for them. Mr Allen was driving the Matron from the hospital about the farm yesterday we all felt very (large hole in paper) used about it, I met them twice when I was selling flags for our day. Mabel and Jim have just been out with ferret but there is no luck with them. I am pleased to hear the war is looking so much better.

With love from us all,
Mother
PS We have had it fine since Monday but it is trying to rain today

Also in the old attic bag was a letter to Allen in France around this time from a female friend back home in Somerset:

Pte A. Green 42915 6th Batt, Dorset's Regt. B.E.F. France

Leighton Sunday Evening

Dear Allen,

Mother gave me your address the last time I was at Chesterblade so I thought I would write to you as I know letters are very welcome at the front. We are pleased to hear you are well and fit. What a lot you will have to tell us when you come home. How nice for you coming across Nelson and some of the boys you know. But I expect you have plenty of new friends by now. Mr Crees and myself have both had the flu or something like it. He was in bed last Sunday and Monday and then I developed the cold and had to go to bed Monday evening till Friday. Silly of me wasn't it? But I'm thankful to say we are both much better. I hope nobody else will have it. Elsie came up from her Aunt Pollie's yesterday to enquire how we were but she was afraid to come in. She told us Aunt Pollie wasn't much better.

It is hard for her being laid up for so long. There is going to be another Whist Drive next month here in aid of the J.M.C.A The same as last year. I expect you remember that one don't you, also three concerts coming off one in aid of the Prisoners War Fund another for the Red X and Mrs Jack Day is giving one in aid of the British Farmer's Red X. Do you know Mr Crees went round with the barrel organ with Jack Fry one night a few weeks ago and we counted the money he collected the other evening and it was over £4. Good wasn't it? Mr Fred Luff is home looking very fit. Mr Crees went shooting with him yesterday. He is coming to have a cup of tea with me one day before he returns. He has 14 days leave. He has been to see Mr Crees' sister at Rouen, this time since he had been over in France: so has a lot to tell us. Aubrey Allen has been home for 2 or 3 days this week but I haven't heard much about Leslie lately. Mr Arthur Allen called here on Wednesday morning to see Mr Crees but I did not see him but Mrs Hoddinot did and thought he was looking wonderfully well considering he only came out of hospital last Monday. He was driving himself. Now I must end up or you will be tired of reading. We all wish you the best of luck and shall be pleased to hear from you when you have time, but always remember to write to Mother first as I know she cannot help feeling anxious about you. Mr Crees says he will write when he can but he is very busy.

Yours very sincerely,
Emmie Crees

The last two letters both talked of various people suffering from flu, so may well have been part of the Spanish Flu pandemic that was omnipresent at the time. The various fundraising for the war effort continued apace as well. The letters from home after all Allen had witnessed as he traversed across war-torn France must have seemed like from another life and a very surreal snapshot of a life once lived. The disparity between country life in

Somerset and the death and destruction in France must have given him a strange sensation.

Driving from Walincourt-Selvigny to Inchy, I passed through Ligny-en-Cambresis, a small village, and the larger town of Caudry, which had large industrial units along its southern edge where I passed through. Caudry would become an important place in Allen's story. He would return there just over a week later, not that he knew this at the time, but in the meantime he was bound for Neuvilly.

4. NEUVILLY

Allen's next diary entry read:

23.10.18 Left Inchy for Nuvilly
24.10.18 Stop a rest to 26.10.18
26.10.18 Left Nuvilly for the reserve lines in dugout fatigues
29.10.18 Went back to Nuvilly for a rest in the barn until 2nd Nov 1918
2.11.18 Left Nuvilly 8 o'clock for…

As said in the last chapter, on leaving the small battle-ruined village of Inchy, Allen travelled to Neuvilly, a small village three miles further east again and lying on the edge of the still German held Mormal Forest. Neuvilly had been temporarily recaptured from the Germans on 10 October 1918 and taken back permanently by the Allies on 17 October. Many of the soldiers who died around this time in the area are buried in the war graves still based in the village today. In 1918, in the ruins of Neuvilly church, a temporary shelter for wounded soldiers was established under the parts of the roof that still survived.

Before this, the French had used the ruined church for a similar purpose. On the back wall behind the alter an intact painting remained showing the ascension of Jesus. It provided some sort of image of faith and hope for the wounded and dying soldiers lying in the beds below.

Wounded US soldiers in Neuvilly Church 26 September 1918

Neuvilly church in 2018

After German submarines sank seven U.S. merchant ships and a telegram was intercepted by the British that revealed Germany was to start financing Mexico's war to recover land from America, the U.S. position of non-intervention changed, and war was declared on Germany on 6 April 1917.

In the old photo of Neuvilly church, the man standing with his hands in his pockets on the left is a twenty-year-old American serviceman named Alfred Hayes. He was an ambulance driver who had been accompanied by a Bouvier de Flanders dog trained to find the wounded still alive on the battlefield. Alfred had been called up from amid the small towns and green, rolling hills and plains of Labette County in South East Kansas. He and his companions were poorly trained and ill equipped but were to provide relief for the war-weary Allied troops. Arriving in France in September 1917, the Americans were short on rations and sleep, and would have entered a scene of mud, burnt and mangled leafless trees; a landscape in which buildings had been left as rubble and roads potholed with shell holes.

Alfred and the other medics searched the battlefields for survivors and transported them first to the triage centre in the ruined church by horse drawn wagon. Once the wounded were stabilised and if they were thought likely to survive their injuries, they were then moved to a hospital in a nearby town. Amongst the rubble of the church, Alfred found a brass crucifix, twelve inches wide and about the same in height, which he kept in his bedroll until the end of the war. During this period serving on the battlefield, and perhaps influenced by the ruined church of St Peter and St Paul in Neuvilly with its ascension of Christ on the shattered wall, Alfred converted to Catholicism. In the region he served in, losses were heavy. The forty-day offensive launched there accounted for more than half the U.S. casualties for the whole war. Of the 1.2 million Americans participating in this offensive, over twenty-six thousand were killed and almost ninety-six thousand wounded.

Alfred survived the war, but on his return home in April 1919, his family disowned him for converting to his wife's religion of Catholicism. He kept with him the brass crucifix and fixed it to the wall by the front door of their home back in the U.S. where it remained for forty-three years. Sadly, Alfred suffered from depression and alcoholism after the war and died from gastric problems related to his drinking at the early age of forty-six. Later, after his wife died, the crucifix was passed down to their daughter and then granddaughter, who in turn hung it on her wall in tribute to her grandfather and those he served with. She vowed, however, to one day return it to the church in Neuvilly from where it came. Nearly ninety years later, she carried out this promise and did indeed return the brass crucifix back to France and to Neuvilly Church, where it still resided at the time of my own visit there in 2018.

Neuvilly was a small settlement with the church in the centre, so Allen would most likely have come across Alfred Hayes and his fellow Americans in the makeshift hospital. Allen stayed in and around Neuvilly for eight days between 26 October and 2 November, lodging in a barn in the village behind the main frontline trenches. Reserve lines were also dug to keep the frontline trenches supplied and as a place of retreat to fight back from if the frontline trenches had to be abandoned while under attack. It appeared from his diary entries that Allen spent some time in the reserve trenches before coming back to Neuvilly to rest again.

Gas and shelling bombardments had been a constant feature in and around Neuvilly and Inchy over the past week of fighting. After the Allies had finally taken Neuvilly back from the Germans three days before Allen's arrival, only a few civilians were still left. The Regimental diary states 'several Germans, mostly wounded, were found hiding in cellars. The village itself was an indescribable mess and the church was badly damaged'. After spending the night in Neuvilly, orders were received on 24 October that Allen's brigade would stay billeted there for a few more days. This time was to be spent resting, training, cleaning billets and reorganising.

The regimental diaries gave further detail about what was happening at this time in Neuvilly. The war was coming to its bitter end following major offensives that summer and autumn, and the U.S. forces coming into the war had given the Allies new impetus. The regimental diary states *'Neuvilly was the climax: what remained was still arduous, but lacked fire. Every man was weary ... To relieve the staleness, Morris Harvey and the Brigade concert party gave excellent entertainments in a barn at Neuvilly: the scenery and gear had been brought up thirty miles from the rear with the aid of a R.A.F. officer.'* This could well have been at the barn that Allen wrote that he was staying in.

My next stop, as Allen's had been, was Neuvilly. I followed his trail in my hire car and found another village with new red brick houses, a town hall and a church that had been repaired since the war. Arriving at noon, I parked in the centre of the village outside the church as young school children filed out of their schoolyard for lunch. Parents held their hands to escort them away for the requisite midday French shut-down when everyone disappears. It was strange seeing the church fully repaired and normal; my only previous views of it had been via old photos on the internet with its side wall blown away. The church doors were open so I went inside and found that it felt strangely familiar. The same large pillars that I had seen in the pictures formed two rows down its centre and the old stone floor slabs held within them a history of the war wounded. The brass crucifix borrowed by Alfred Hayes stood on an alter and could have told a thousand stories.

Neuvilly in February 2018

Back outside the church, I could hear a distorted French voice approaching through a loudhailer and this broke the midday quiet of France with a shock. Around the bend in the road, a red car drove by with brightly coloured writing advertising a French circus troupe. Out of the loudhailer fixed to the roof, the voice spoke excitedly about the circus which would be arriving tomorrow. As the car disappeared from view, I could hear it move around the village streets, laying its bait. Tied to a sign post across the road, a poster advertised the shows for tomorrow and the next day in bright colours. The church enjoyed an elevated position and when I looked over its wall I saw the bright reds and yellows of a circus tent erected on a village green and new-looking lorries. On a muddy patch to the side, camels and llamas were tied up to a rail with nets of hay for them to pick from. The noise and colour of the circus seemed at odds with the otherwise sleepy quiet of Neuvilly and like another world from the rubble and destruction of the war. As I looked across the town, I tried to imagine Allen's time here. In contrast to the heavy, bleak atmosphere around Albert and Bapaume, where it was possible to imagine its wartime horror, the peace of a place like Neuvilly today made it hard to imagine it in 1918. That it had been able to return to this tranquillity seemed reassuring for humanity.

On 26 October, Allen and his battalion left Neuvilly at 8.45am and headed for Vendegies-au-Bois where they stopped to eat lunch, before leaving at 2pm for Poix-du-Nord where they were to provide support for the troops already there. They arrived at 4.30pm and experienced gas shelling that night. Further ahead of them, forward Allied forces had been attacking Englefontaine where they had encountered machine gun fire and gas, as well as counter-attacks on their outposts. The next day, 27 October, the Dorsets were reported as being employed in a *'brigade support'* role, 'just north of Poix-du-Nord'. Records state that it was a *'Quiet day with shelling at night'*.

In Poix-du-Nord itself, persistent shelling at night was recorded, often involving gas, while around Englefontaine, a heavy enemy barrage at 6am was followed by an enemy attack. Twelve Allied soldiers were captured before the enemy were eventually driven back.

Allen continued the next day, 28 October, in brigade support at the same location north of Poix-du-Nord. The weather was described as *'fine'* and his A Company was one of two working parties. The other working party suffered casualties, with one shell alone reported to have killed ten Allied troops. Regimental diaries reported that *'Enemy aeroplanes were exceedingly active throughout the day, as was enemy artillery. In the evening Poix-du-Nord was shelled. Our artillery kept up harassing fire throughout the night. In consequence of the enemy shelling of forward villages and casualties to the civilian population, these villages were ordered to be evacuated and a great many civilians were cleared during the day'.*

On the following day, 29 October, the weather was again recorded as *'fine'* and Allen's company suffered eight casualties from one shell early in the morning. They were relieved in the afternoon by another battalion and then headed back to billets in Neuvilly once more. The battalion travelled via tracks south of Vendegies-au-Bois and Ovillers, but north of Amerval. Once east of Ovillers, they were instructed to *'move by Platoons, and if a road is touched (by aeroplanes or shelling), troops will march in file'.*

Billeted back in Neuvilly, they spent 30 October training, reorganising and undergoing inspections. On 31 October, the log says: *'CO holds a kit inspection in the morning, with baths in the afternoon. Also in the afternoon, a football match was played against the East Yorks, who won 5 goals to nil'.* On 1 November, the Dorsets stayed in reserve and billeted in Neuvilly with *'training in the morning and all Officers and NCOs have a lecture by the GOC in the afternoon on "Wood Fighting". Warning order received that Battalion would move to Vendegies-au-Bois on the 2nd.'* An Allied patrol nearby managed to establish an outpost and rescue thirty-four civilians from a house in what had been No Man's Land up until then, and brought them back to safety.

On 2 November, the weather was *'dull, with a lot of rain'* and the battalion left Neuvilly at 8pm and headed for Vendegies-au-Bois, parading in Company order. Battalion Orders were *'dress will be full marching order. Route by tracks North of Amerval and Ovillers. Intervals of 100 yards between Platoons. Transport, where possible, will move by tracks. If moving by road they will conform to traffic routes already laid down. Companies are reminded that when moving by road, they will march in file'.* Allen billeted in Vendegies-au-Bois that night. The nearby Poix-du-Nord endured heavy shelling during the night.

The lanes and countryside around Vendegies-au-Bois, similar to Somerset

Vendegies-au-Bois, Poix-du-Nord, Amerval, Ovillers and Englefontaine were all small settlements within a seven mile area to the north-east of Neuvilly so I headed off in my car to trace Allen's journey to these places. This area suddenly looked very familiar and it could have been somewhere in Somerset. The wide open spaces of crops had been replaced with hedgerows and trees alongside country lanes, and smaller sized fields of grass where livestock would be grazing in the summer. In Vendegies-au-Bois, I came across a line of British war graves set within a communal French graveyard around the red brick village church.

British war graves in Vendegies-au-Bois churchyard

The next village, Poix-du-Nord, was more boisterous with students from a college messing around in the street and tractors going up and down the road. The walled British war cemetery sat adjacent to a French graveyard, which followed the normal French custom of gravel pathways and family tombstones rather than the more English grass and headstones. Next, Englefontaine had a large main road passing through it like Inchy, and attractive lines of pollard trees near the church gave it a pleasant village feel. All these places were so quiet. Only the war cemeteries were a reminder of how this countryside had once been ravaged by war. The British war cemetery in Englefontaine was down a side street and a sign pointed visitors down a narrow grass pathway between a house on the left and a smallholder's property on the right. As I walked down the grass pathway wet from drizzle, a couple of rough haired ponies on my right walked across their mud-pocked paddock to say hello. Elsewhere amongst the ramshackle collection of homemade sheds, scrap cars and machinery, chickens poked around an old tractor in a muddy yard and a dog eyed me suspiciously. At the end of the pathway, the now familiar sight of a walled British war cemetery appeared, extending in an L-shape around the border of the smallholding.

Englefontaine church and war memorial

It was getting late after a long day travelling, so I headed for the only place where I could find accommodation in the area just north of Englefontaine in Pont a Vaches, which roughly translates as 'cow bridge' which seems highly appropriate for a farmer. My hosts at La Chaumière appeared from a large farmhouse to the side of a gravel driveway and took me down to the accommodation at the bottom of the track. I thought I had booked a room in a hotel so I was surprised to find I had actually got one of four bedrooms with a communal kitchen in a self-built chalet. There was also an indoor swimming pool and hot tub next to the kitchen. Large glass sliding doors looked out onto a grass field with a small lake and a forest in the distance behind it. I was told French singing stars were staying the day before and I was left to settle in. A little later, at the suggestion of my hosts, I headed into Le Quesnoy, a town just to the north, for an evening meal at Chez Ahmed, a Moroccan restaurant. In faltering French I ordered a chicken dish and in due course a lamb dish appeared but it may well have been my fault and the thought of trying to rectify the situation in French resigned me to my lamb fate.

I awoke early the next morning and soaked up the picturesque view through the glass doors that extended right across one wall of the bedroom. After studying the map for my day's travels, tracing Allen's next movements, I realised that the view from my room looked out across the exact part of the Mormal Forest where I would be going that day. Breakfast arrived in the kitchen and the wife of the couple who ran the property joined me at the table. It soon became evident that both my French and her English were of an equally bad standard, so we used a combination of pointing, talking loudly and using an internet translator on my laptop computer. Over fresh croissants and strong coffee I talked with my host about my journey across France tracing my great uncle's war experience and the book I'm writing. I was surprised when she began to tell me of her dismay that today's French people don't appreciate and commemorate enough the sacrifice that was made by soldiers a hundred years ago. When I suggested that maybe this was because they wanted to forget the horror of what happened, she disagreed and thought it was just a simple lack of appreciation of the sacrifice that was made on their behalf by many other countries. I reflected on this; it had certainly been noticeable that aside from the memorials and cemeteries maintained by Commonwealth countries, especially by Britain and Australia, there was not much evidence in the places I had visited of memorials or museums maintained by the French. I felt surprised; given this was the centenary year of the Armistice. My host told me her father had been a member of the Resistance in the Second World War. Once breakfast was over, I headed back onto the road to continue in Allen's footsteps.

The view of the Mormal Forest from my room at La Chaumière

5. The Final Battle of the War

On 3 November 1918, the weather was *'dull but dry'* and orders were received at 3pm that the battalion would be moving forward the next day and launch an attack on the enemy in the Mormal Forest. Allen's A Company was to leave Vendegies-au-Bois at 2.10am. Initially, an artillery formation would be adopted, which would then be superseded by a wood fighting formation. Preceding the attack would be an artillery barrage and as the attack progressed, this barrage line would advance at one hundred metres every six minutes. The Company at the front of the attack would light two red flares on demand from contact aeroplanes.

Allen's A Company would have contained three hundred men and, alongside another three hundred men in each of B, C and D Company, these made up the 50th Brigade of some twelve hundred men. Within his three hundred-strong A Company, he would have been in a platoon of forty men, and within this platoon he would have been in a section of eight men commanded by a lance corporal. This group of eight men would have been an established, tight-knit group and difficult for a young, inexperienced new recruit to enter into. Each man would need to trust the others with his life, and this trust had to be earned as new recruits could not always be relied on due to their inexperience. In essence, it was a baptism of fire that Allen was plunged into, as the old stagers already in the Section would not yet trust him in a scenario of extreme danger.

There is another letter in the Dorothy Bag written home by Allen whilst in Neuvilly, and dated 3 November 1918, the day before the attack through the Mormal Forest would take place.

3rd Nov 1918 42915 Green 16th platoon D. Company
6th Dorsets B.E.F. France

Dear Mother,

I have now received three letters from you the last one written on the 25th, I was pleased you put in part of the journal. I am glad to hear that Mr Allen is out of hospital and is getting on and are surprised to hear that he drives out the Matron, do you think they are going to make a match of it. I wrote to Auntie P sorry to hear that she is so ill. I am still back from the line but do not know how we shall stop there. I am still with my old mates and Cary but have not heard any more of P. Green or Perkins or any of the rest of them. Have you sent on a cake yet but it is no good to send any butter or cheese and can you put in a writing pad and envelopes not to big and a piece of soap. We cannot buy anything out here. I would send home some of my money if I can get half a chance. I have not much more to tell you this time. I hope you are all quite well as it leaves me the same.

Now I must close with love to you all from Allen.
Tell Jim I will write to him next time.

Reading the *Shepton Mallet Journal* that week with its pages of Somerset cattle sales and local stories must have seemed a million miles away for Allen amongst the rubble of France as he prepared for an attack through the Mormal Forest.

The Regimental diary described how the battle developed the next day, 4 November: 'Meanwhile the front had reached the western edge of Mormal Forest:

on entering it, the direction of the Division would once more be due east. It seems hard that any further efforts should have been demanded: for on October 27th Marshal Foch was authorized to receive German representatives and hand them the terms of the Armistice. The last battle the Division fought was the first of its kind. It had fought in woods, and held horrible recollections of what that entailed: but it had never advanced fighting through one. What happened turned out to be evil enough, but less evil than anticipated. The trees were singular oaks and beeches; parts had been cleared for timber: in parts there was dense undergrowth. Tracks intersected one another, but at an angle to the line of advance. In the centre was the village of Locquignol. The advertisement of La Chenie, a "grand hotel-restaurant for tourists and walkers," proclaimed it an ideal place for tired town-dwellers to recover their strength, and the Spirit Ironic had inserted a poet's fourteen stanzas in praise of its beauty and its quiet, together with charming photographs.

"D'autres bruits de combats ont troublé mon silence,
Et des troupes en marche ont foulé mes gazons
En des âges de haine et d'âpre violence,
Ou la guerre hurlait parmi mes frondaisons."

The past had come back to life.'

The poem translates as:

Sounds of combat disturb my silence,
And marching troops trample my lawns
And in times of hatred and violence,
War screams amongst my foliage.

The Mormal Forest on 30 October 1918 prior to the attack

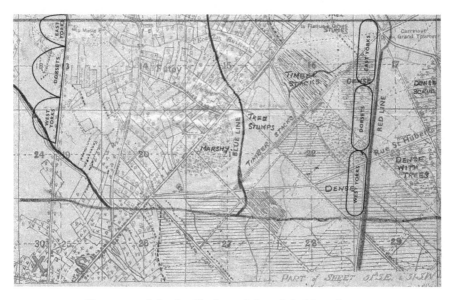

The regimental plan for Allen's attack through the Mormal Forest

(reproduced by kind permission of The Keep Museum, Dorchester)

The Regimental diary continues:

'Nov. 4th. The forest the Division attacked with all three brigades: it was part of a thrust on a front of twenty-five miles by the 1st, 3rd and 4th Armies. The 52nd led at 5.30 a.m. and gained the first line, with heavy losses: the 51st followed and, suffering fewer casualties than they had from shell-fire in the assembly, reached their appointed line by 10.40 a.m. The 50th Brigade were to pass through both. The Dorsets were in the centre, and had started moving from Vendegies at 2.10 in the morning: by 4 a.m. they were at their first place of assembly, where they halted for four and a half hours: by 9.20 a.m. at the second, and at the third by 11.45 a.m. The attack began for them at 1 p.m., with "A" and "D" Companies in front, "C" in support and "B" in reserve. Two sections of the Machine-gun Company and one section of the Light Trench Mortar Battery accompanied them. Each man carried two days' rations and two water bottles. Every two hundred yards direction was checked by compass, 2/Lieut. K. D. Marshall being directing officer, and trees were blazed continually as the Battalion moved forward. No real barrage was possible: but our own 18-pounders fired short and caused sixteen casualties, and promiscuous shells brought tree and branches crashing down (One 5-ft. 6-ins. in diameter very nearly crushed the Brigadier and Brigade-Major). By 2.10 p.m. an advance of nearly a mile had been made, and several machine-guns captured. This had to be done by individual leading and outflanking. At 3.30 p.m. the advance was held up till dusk by fire from the Institut Forestier and from Locquignol ... The advance stopped just beyond the third objective ... but two thousand yards short of the final mark ... When darkness came, and it was very thick, and the rain was streaming down, the line ran roughly north and south, east of the Institut Forestier, but with Locquignol still untaken. The Brigade planned to attack this spot, but just before the time arranged the Division ordered a definite line to be reported, and Captain Barber had hard work to communicate with battalions.

'*Nov. 5th. At midnight, however, patrols found Locquignol deserted … The losses in reaching the forest had been five men killed, forty-two wounded, and in the fighting seven killed, thirty-three wounded and one missing … This was the last fighting of the 50th Brigade. It was well that success crowned its final effort. The Division had captured one hundred and forty-four machine-guns and fifteen field guns, and the prisoners came from no less than sixteen different regiments.*

The Dorsets retired into billets in Locquignol by 3 p.m. and tried to get dry after the soaking in the forest. All ranks were very, very tired … But the work done was enough: the war was won. As its share in the last three months the 3rd Army had won eighteen decisive battles, driven the enemy back over sixty miles of country, and captured sixty-seven thousand prisoners and eight hundred guns

The section of the Mormal Forest now where Allen's platoon fought through

… On the 10th the order was given that soft caps would be worn: in the evening they had a concert. Official news of the Armistice arrived at 8.30 a.m. on the 11th:

at 11 o'clock all firing was to cease. The Battalion had breakfast and paraded at 9.45; the Commanding Officer read out the notice and three cheers were given for the King. Just that: survivors might shake one another's hand for having lived through it, but their first thoughts were for those who had fallen: to other emotions they were dead. It was left to London to make a noise. Overtasked nature cried out for rest and sleep. The work of the soldiers was done.'

Setting off from my idyllic accommodation in the hire car, I drove the short distance to the edge of the woodland where Allen's platoon had entered into the Mormal Forest on 4 November 1918. After billeting in Vendegies-au-Bois for the night, at 2.10am Allen moved off at the start of the attack. They progressed another two and a half miles from Vendegies-au-Bois to the edge of the Mormal Forest where I now took up Allen's trail once more. As I entered into the trees I tried to imagine what it would have been like on that day in November a hundred years ago with rain and Allied shells falling down around them, machine gun fire, and trees ablaze and splintering branches striking the ground. It felt surreal walking into the same woodland a hundred years later. There was not another soul around. The forest was still made up of beech and oak trees regenerated from the beech nuts and acorns dropped onto the forest floor from trees that had been destroyed in warfare. The forest was huge, measuring just under twenty-five thousand acres in size. I felt the solemn history of the place as I slowly tramped through the undergrowth towards Locquignol two and a half miles away in the middle of the forest.

Following the same route as the attack, I jumped across a number of streams and rivers and negotiated areas of swamp. Deer were a frequent sight and at one point I encountered a herd of ten of them trailing through the trees. I cut across a succession of long, straight, man-made tracks that extended away at right angles to my direction of travel, then stopped and rested at various points I had marked on my map where Allen's platoon had also stopped after reaching various military objectives. The only sign of human life I encountered were two forestry workers cutting up wood with chainsaws in the near distance at one point. I bypassed them unnoticed. The character of the forest changed along the way, varying between thick young undergrowth to older, taller trees thinned out over time.

After an hour and a half, more light started to appear through the trees ahead and I knew Locquignol could not be far off now. As I reached the edge of the forest and stepped through into the open winter sunshine, I felt I had passed through a portal to Allen's experience while walking the route taken by his regiment in their last battle of the war. The last battle in four years of insanity for humankind.

Between the forest and the village, there was a field of pasture. As I began to cross it, I noticed two homemade shooting perches built adjacent to the hedgerows, probably for the boar hunting that was popular around this forest region. I climbed up the wobbly ladder of one of these ramshackle wooden shacks. On the platform at the top, around three metres up, was an old stool slowly rotting in the weather and a small, makeshift table made out of a wooden box. Where once snipers and machine gunners aimed fire at enemy troops, now aiming fire was done for sport and leisure. It felt eerie being in a sniper position facing the forest and I continued making my way towards Locquignol. It was mid-morning by now, and a sleepy lull covered the village like a blanket. An elderly man pottered around his garden and the occasional car drove by on its way through the forest. The café and tabac were both closed as I arrived at the communal cemetery, which held a solitary British war grave. I perched on the graveyard wall next to the familiar Portland stone gravestone and ate the packed lunch I had brought with me. It read 'A SOLDIER OF THE GREAT WAR. DORSETSHIRE REGIMENT. AUG 1914. KNOWN UNTO GOD'. Snowdrops had been planted at its base. This lone grave of an unknown soldier from Allen's regiment right at the beginning of the war formed some kind of apt bookend as it was in the same spot the Dorsetshire Regiment would end the war too. It felt like a sad reflection on a war with a frontline that groaned back and forth short distances and always ended up back where it started, achieving nothing but the mass destruction and slaughter left in its wake.

PART FIVE
THE AFTERMATH

1. Armistice Day

In October 1918, the Germans had approached U.S. President Woodrow Wilson seeking an armistice to end the war. They hoped for lenient terms. When this became general knowledge, the German public became outraged and wanted to know why they were still fighting. The Kaiser was forced to abdicate to avert a revolution and the terms of the armistice became harsher during the negotiations. Soldiers in the German Army had increasingly begun to desert their posts and sailors at sea mutinied once they realised they faced impossible odds. Production back in Germany to supply the war effort had reduced due to striking workers and all these factors gave rise to the period now known as the German Revolution.

Together with the British Prime Minister David Lloyd George and French Premier Georges Clemenceau, the U.S. signed an Armistice Treaty with Germany on 11 November 1918 that ended fighting on the Western Front. Defeated and humiliated, the Germans were forced to retreat from occupied territory and surrender weapons, aeroplanes and ships. Sixty-five million people from thirty countries had been involved in fighting in the planet's first truly world war across Europe, the Middle East, Africa and Asia. Revolution in Russia in 1917 had led to the end of the Imperial Government and the rise of the Bolshevik Party to power, led by Lenin.

In total, over eighteen million people had died and twenty-three million had been wounded. Around eleven million had died in the military, with three-quarters of a million of these being British, and one hundred and eighty-eight thousand from British colonies. Six million civilians had also lost their lives. In previous wars, the majority of deaths during conflicts had been due to disease, but this time two-thirds of deaths came from direct battle. Average life expectancy in the trenches was just six weeks, and this was a lot lower if you were a stretcher bearer or young officer. One third of deaths, however, still came from disease, such as the flu pandemic in 1918, and many had died from disease while being held as a prisoner of war.

The war bore witness to a huge amount of change and innovation over the four years. At the beginning of the war, attacks had been carried out by generals on horseback with charging men on foot in cloth caps and armed with rifles with no covering fire. This had been replaced by the end with steel-helmeted teams making dashes forward with covering fire from waves of artillery shells. Weapons at their disposal now included grenades, flame throwers and portable machine guns. Aeroplanes had become sophisticated in combat and were armed with wireless radio as they fought duels in the sky. Tanks had been used for the first time.

So, at the eleventh hour, of the eleventh day, of the eleventh month in 1918, the Armistice officially began and was greeted with jubilation across Britain. Wild celebrations ensued and in London there were accounts of wild abandon that would have been unthinkable during the war. Unrestrained drinking, dancing and sexual promiscuity abounded, and there was singing, cheering and the waving of flags to celebrate. Locally, the *Shepton Mallet Journal* described the atmosphere in Wells:

'There was a complete transformation in the appearance of the city ... streets and buildings were suddenly decorated with flags, the Cathedral bells rang, and there was a general air of rejoicing ... it was decided a public meeting should be called for the afternoon. Consequently, at three o'clock, the market place was crowded with citizens and children of the schools (two schools had only re-opened

in the morning on account of the influenza epidemic), and the Cadet Corps of the Wells Boys' Blue School, with their bugle band, marched from the schools to the Market Place.'

All around the country, families and friends waited to welcome home their loved ones back from far flung places on land and sea where they had fought. News of what had happened to them over the last few days of fighting and when they would be returning was awaited with baited breath. So, what news was there of Allen?

As part of A Company in the Dorsets' 50th Brigade, we know from the Regimental diaries that Allen travelled east from Neuvilly on 3 November five miles or so to Vendegies-au-Bois inside the Mormal Forest. Just north of here they paraded at a crossroads at 2.10am on 4 November and enemy shells caused eight casualties. They marched north-east and after nearly two hours under the cover of night and in torrential rain, they reached their first assembly point north-east of Poix-au-Nord at 4am, and halted there for four and a half hours. Moving off again at 8.30am, the Company travelled along the Englefontaine-Louvignies Road and reach their second assembly point at 9.20am and their third at 11.45am. *'This was impeded by a barrage fired by our own guns apparently in answer to a red smoke bomb dropped by an aeroplane'* close by. *'The barrage continued ... from 12 noon to 12.30pm; it was luckily mostly behind our assembly position but caused some casualties to the Dorsets ... (who) waited ... for an hour to allow the artillery to move-up'.*

For Allen's A Company, their attack proper began at 1pm, and they led at the front of the attack through the forest alongside D Company, accompanied by machine gunners and trench mortar fire. *'In the centre and on the left, it was not possible to recognize a barrage line. One or two batteries on the left fired consistently short from 1pm to 2.30pm ... 18 Pounders put down a heavy barrage on the Dorsets leading Companies causing a number of casualties'.*

After just over an hour, they had advanced a mile and after two and a half hours the advance stopped and was held up until darkness descended again. Shelling from the Allied 18-pounder guns had caught trees ablaze, and brought branches crashing down around them, killing sixteen of their own men.

2. A Telegram

Out of the old bag in the attic, there was a telegram dated on Armistice Day:

Office of Origin 6 HMS (--)

To Mr S. Green, Banks Farm, Chesterblade, Shepton Mallet

11.11.18

Regret your son 42915 Private A.J. Green 6th Dorsets Died 5th November at 3 Casualty Clearing station France gunshot wounds chest. The army council express their sympathy 1/62 Records

On the day the country celebrated the end of the war, my family received the news that every family dreaded; Allen had been killed in the last battle. The telegram was short and to the point and must have been devastating news to receive on the day people were celebrating the end of the war. It would have been an agonising wait for the family between each letter received home from Allen and after his last letter from him written on 3 November, there would have been no way of knowing how he was until the dreadful telegram arrived on Armistice Day. Allen signed off his final letter with the words 'Tell Jim I will write to him next time'. My grandfather, then an eleven-year-old boy, must have been terribly shaken by the death of his big brother. The bond and warmth between them was evident in Allen's letters home. What a tragic waste this would now be no more.

The *Shepton Mallet Journal* described the day in the local village of Evercreech:

'*There was a general display of flags and bunting. The Church bells rang out joyful peals at intervals during the day; also in honour and in memory of the fallen, a solemn knell and muffled peals were rung, during which the Union Jack was at half-mast. In the evening there was a combined service of thanksgiving, and "In Memoriam" held in the Parish Church, a very large congregation being present. The vicar ... read the roll of honour for the Parish, with the addition of Allen Green, for it was known but by a very few present that Mr. and Mrs. Sidney Green of Chesterblade, had heard only the same day the sad intelligence of the death of their son from wounds in France.*'

From the Regimental diaries, we can track Allen's movements and a further tragedy of his death is that he was in combat action for such a short time before his untimely death. His friend Cary, mentioned at various times in his letters, survived the war and many years later spoke to my father about my great uncle at a farming social event they were both attending. My father, who was named Allen by my grandfather in memory of his older brother, said Cary explained he was with Allen when he was wounded by shrapnel from the Allied shells that were falling short, so was probably in Allen's eight-man Section. Allen was not killed by gunshot wounds to the chest as the telegram informed, although I suppose this was a less difficult reason to give than admitting your own shells had fallen short and killed your own soldiers. As I walked through the Mormal Forest that day following Allen's path, I stopped at the point where he fell and reflected for a while on his life and all that he had witnessed. From the forest floor, I picked up six acorns and decided there and then to bring them back to his home in Chesterblade and plant them on the farm as part of a new memorial wood in his memory. I hoped in some way this would bring him back home to where he belonged.

After becoming wounded in the Mormal Forest by shrapnel from the Allied bombs, Allen would have been carried by Field Ambulance stretcher bearers to an Aid Post where he would have been given some initial medical attention and assessed by the Battalion Medical Officer. Stretcher bearers could administer some nominal first aid, but their main task was to get the injured out of the line of fire. The Aid Posts were normally positioned just behind the front line and formed the first stage of the two hundred and forty man strong self-contained Field Ambulance unit. This unit marched to where the action was with its own supplies, medical staff, cooks, clerks, wagons, horses and motor vehicles.

A typical Field Ambulance

From the Aid Post, he would have been moved by stretcher bearers to a tented Advanced Dressing Station in Englefontaine, where he would have been further diagnosed and assessed.

From here, Allen would then have been transferred five miles back to the Main Dressing Station at Forest-en-Cambresis, where his injuries would have been attended to. Once he was in a condition good enough to travel, he was moved to Number 3 Casualty Clearing Station (CCS) at Caudry, a further nine miles back, and at this point he left the care of the Field Ambulance unit. My great uncle could not have known when he passed through Caudry on 22 October that he would return here on 4 November to die.

Number 3 CCS was based in a building the Germans had been using as a hospital for most of the war until Caudry was retaken by the Allies on 10 October 1918. Caudry had been used by the Germans as a main operational base throughout the war, and there were twenty thousand German soldiers stationed here in a town of twelve thousand local French citizens.

The building in Caudry where Number 3 Casualty Clearing Station was located in 1918

A CCS was a larger, better equipped and more permanently established medical facility, and its role was as a staging post to treat and get less serious cases back to their unit. They were usually equipped with around twenty operating theatres, with half of these in use at a time, with twelve surgical teams rotating shifts. Upon entering the CCS, Allen would have had his condition examined and been stripped of his bloodstained and dirty khaki and put into Red Cross pyjamas. At this point his belongings would have been put into the handmade cloth Dorothy Bag that would eventually turn up again in an attic in 2011. He would then have been carried by stretcher to a dressing room and put on one of ten tables there. Another medical officer would have then attended to his injuries and assigned him to a particular ward or straight to an operating theatre, depending on the injury.

Maud McCarthy, the Matron-in-Chief of the British Expeditionary Force, was the only official to hold a position for the entire war, and her official war diaries are held in the National Archives. Her job had been to manage and inspect all the medical facilities in France. Her entry on 5 November 1918 when Allen was at Number 3 CCS in Caudry includes:

'Then on to No.3 CCS Miss Ruck, TFNS Sister in charge, Lt. Col. Reay, OC. This Unit was also in an enormous building. They were extremely busy, with only 6 Nurses, and I undertook during the day to send the remainder of her Staff who had been scattered in other CCSs. Everyone was doing their utmost. The Staff were accommodated in a fine Chateau quite close. There was every convenience, except that there were no windows anywhere'.

At this time, casualty numbers were soaring because the frontline was moving. The National Archives in Kew hold copies of the Admission and Discharge Books for Field Service for Number 3 CCS where Allen was admitted. I went to look at the records held for the time when Allen was there. The columns in the books recorded the name and rank of the patient, the wounds and injuries inflicted, and date of admission, discharge, or death. The records for Allen's CCS in Caudry seem to have stopped on 25 October 1918, at the point when Number 3 CCS left its location at Beaulencourt and moved to Caudry, and they started again in the next book on 9 November 1918. Around forty wounded soldiers were admitted every day in the records at this point. I then discovered a few more written pages in isolation at the back of the book that covered operations carried out over the period from 4 November 1918, the day Allen had been admitted, up until 8 November 1918. Some typical records included *'Bullet removed: Brachial artery found divided and ligatured'* and *'Blown off left forearm amputated'*. A number of prisoners of war are recorded to have been operated on amongst the Allied injured.

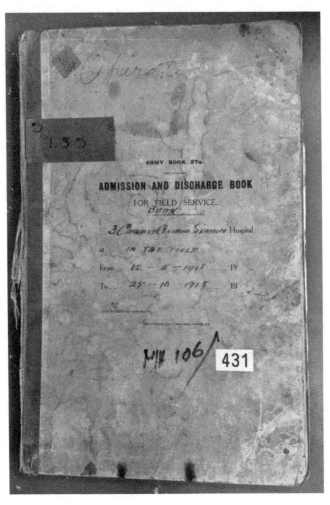

The CCS Admission and Discharge book where Allen had been hospitalised

I scanned through the records and around sixty operations took place on 4 November, the day Allen had been admitted, and another sixty operations on 5 November, the day he died, but I couldn't see Allen's name anywhere. We will never know, therefore, what exactly happened to him at that point, but we can probably presume his injuries were so bad that he faced no hope of recovery by operation. It may be that he died in the early hours not long after being admitted, although it is strange why only operations were recorded between 4 and 8 November and the other admissions were not recorded in the normal way as before.

Of the survivors, the worst cases were treated and moved back to Base Hospitals or back to the UK, whilst for others like Allen with fatal wounds, the CCS would be where they would die. Many CSS, therefore, have a war grave cemetery nearby, as is the case in Caudry where Allen is buried. Caudry had three CCS based in the town and the cemetery contains seven hundred and thirteen war graves from between 1914 to 1918, with casualties from Britain, New Zealand, Australia, India, Canada, France, China, Germany and Italy. Fifty of these remain unidentified.

Caudry cemetery, 1918

A Graves Registration Report Form from 1918 records the location of Allen's grave:

ADDENDA COMPREHENSIVE REPORT.   Army Form W. 8372.

GRAVES REGISTRATION REPORT FORM.

REPORT No. 3   SCHEDULE No. 42/a.

Commune : CAUDRY.

PLACE OF BURIAL   CAUDRY BRITISH CEMETERY.

Map Reference   57b.J.19.a.9.1.

The following are buried here :—   This Report Caudry   Sch. 33/c. - 44/c.
                                   Sameils Report Caudry   Sch. 1/c. - 11/c.

Regiment	No.	Name	Rank and Initials	Date of Death	Cross Erected or G. R. U'd.	Plot, Row and Grave
		PLOT 4, ROW 'H'. Contd.				
14/Welsh Regt.	73857	EVANS	Pte. D.J.	5/11/18	E	17
155/Army Bde. R.F.A.	5831	POOLE	Dvr. T.B.	do.	E	18
13/Rifle Brigade	13309	BISHOP	Rfn. G.	do.	E	19
9/West Ridings	52074	McLOUGHLIN	Pte. M.H.	4/11/18	E	20
4/Royal Fus.	100016	DUCK	Pte. W.K.	do.	E	21
R. Welsh Fus.	15698	LUDLOW	L/Cpl. E.T.	5/11/18	E	22
37/M. G. Batt.	5990	STRATTON	Sgt. A.J.	4/11/18	I.W.G.C.	23
6/Dorset Regt.	153888	DART	Pte. H.	5/11/18	E	24
do.	42915	GREEN	Pte. A.	do.	E	25
7/Sherwoods	1017827	GOULDBY	Pte. G.	do.	E	26
6/Dorset Regt.	41868	FEARMAN	Pte. A.	do.	E	27
A. S. Corps	R/357182	ROSS	Pte. A.	do.	E	28
9/West Ridings	22852	OLIVER	Sgt. W.	do.	E	29

ENTERED

CHECKED

Allen's Grave Registration Form

Allen had already been dead for six days when the family were finally
informed of his death on 11 November, Armistice Day. It seemed to me
such a waste of a life and a pointless death, especially when you consider
that the Armistice was in the process of being drawn up towards the end
of October. Why continue to send people to their death when the war

had already come to an end in effect? Why take a country boy of eighteen years of age away from a farm where he was producing food the country so desperately needed? After weeks of training since June, what had been the point of going into battle for a few days and dying pretty much instantly by shelling from his own side? How does any of that make any sense?

This story wasn't one of heroism amidst the horrors of war in the muddy and bloody trenches of the battlefield. There was no stoic survival or honourable death. It was just the story of a pointless death that didn't need to happen and served no real purpose other than to take a son and brother away from a family. What a shame this young man would never grow up to live a life, whatever that would hold.

There was another letter to Allen's family in the Dorothy Bag from one of Allen's friends he mentioned in his letters. This was received just over a week after the telegram from the army.

Letter 43048
1 platoon
A Camp
5ᵗʰ Batt Dorsets,
BEF France
20.11.18 France

Dear Mr and Mrs Green and family,
It is with much regret that I write to express my sympathy to you all in your sad loss. I cannot hardly realize it's true, poor kid he was a pal always. It terribly upset me when I knew I had to leave him at the base and more still when I found I couldn't go into the same battalion, true we can't all be lucky but I do wish Alan could have been spared but I hope no doubt he is better off than us but we can't see it, I know just how the feeling is, the same as you know happened to us when Alec was killed.

I heard the news from home. I wrote to him and I know now why I didn't get a reply.
It has quite upset me I can assure you. I am at a place just off Mons don't know a
bit where the 6th Batt has been or is now. So I'm sorry I can't help you in finding out
any details whatever, again expressing my deepest sympathy
I remain
Yrs sincerely,
Percy Green

So, it would appear that other than receiving the news of his death by army
telegram on 11 November, there had been no other contact from anyone to
provide any more details of his death. In the attic bag, the next contact from
the army wasn't until five months later in March 1919.

Official Form
No 16352 Army Form B 104-121
No 2 Record Office
Exeter
25.3.1919

Sir,
In continuation of the notification sent to you regarding the death of the late
No 42915 Pte A.J. Green
Regiment 6th Batn Dorset Regt
I beg to inform you that an official report has now been received that the late soldier
is buried at Caudry Cer: Military Cemetery, 5 miles west-north-west of Le Chateau.
Yours faithfully,
J.H. Hall
Colonel in charge of records No 8 District
Officer in charge of records Exeter

The King commands me to assure you of the true sympathy of His Majesty and The Queen in your sorrow.

He whose loss you mourn died in the noblest of causes. His Country will be ever grateful to him for the sacrifice he has made for Freedom and Justice.

Milner

Secretary of State for War.

𝔉or 𝔎ing & 𝔆ountry

A letter from the King

It must have been difficult to grieve for a dead son and brother without knowing much about the events surrounding his death, and without a body to bury. The last time the family had seen Allen would have been at the beginning of October before he made the crossing to France. They had not been able to lay flowers on a grave and he had been buried in a place miles across the sea which they had never visited and had no knowledge of.

It must have been all so hard to comprehend. If his birthday had been a few months later he would not have been old enough for conscription. The two communications from the army via telegram offer nothing but the short, sharp facts of the matter, and completely lack any kind of solace or empathy.

Another envelope was produced out of the Dorothy bag. It was edged in black and had two union jack flags in the centre under which 'For King & Country' was written. Inside was a letter with a crest at the top.

At least this official communication offered some comfort.

A memorial service was held for Allen in St Mary's Chapel in Chesterblade. In the Dorothy Bag were two black-edged cards from the service.

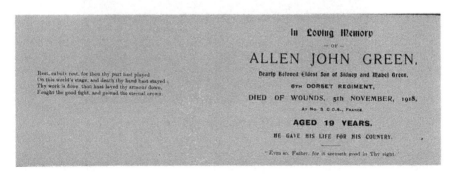

In Loving Memory
— of —
ALLEN JOHN GREEN,
Dearly Beloved Eldest Son of Sidney and Mabel Green,
6TH DORSET REGIMENT,
DIED OF WOUNDS, 5th NOVEMBER, 1918,
AT No. 3 C.C.S., FRANCE
AGED 19 YEARS.
HE GAVE HIS LIFE FOR HIS COUNTRY.

"Even so, Father, for it seemeth good in Thy sight."

Rest, exultly rest, for thou thy part hast played
On this world's stage, and death thy hand hast stayed ;
Thy work is done, thou hast layed thy armour down,
Fought the good fight, and gained the eternal crown.

Allen's memorial service card

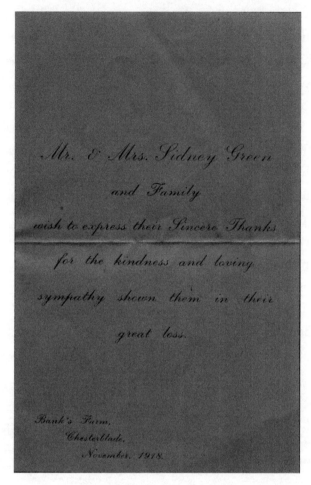

Allen's memorial service card

Inside St. Mary's Chapel in Chesterblade, a plaque was erected on the wall in remembrance of Allen. It is still there today and reads:

In Memorium
Pte. Allen John Green
6th Dorset Regt.

Died of Wounds in France
Nov. 5th 1918. Aged 19 Years

Their Life for their Country
No man can do more

I've sat in this ancient chapel in Chesterblade many times over the years and have tried to imagine what it would have been like for the village to sit here a hundred years ago, as the congregation mourned one of their own who had died and was now buried across the Channel in France. I have thought back to the time I sat here in 1992 aged nineteen and we were gathered in the Chapel for the funeral of my grandfather, Allen's younger brother, Jim, who had died at the age of eighty-five. I had been the same age as Allen when he died and I imagined being in his shoes and experiencing the things he witnessed. I imagined being conscripted into the army and cycling five hours back and forth on leave from a windswept army camp on the hillside behind Chesil Beach in Wyke Regis. I imagined myself dressed in a scratchy, khaki army uniform. I imagined catching the train to Folkestone and being served tea and cakes in the Mole Café by Margaret and Florence Jeffery. I imagined sailing on a ship for the first time in my life and arriving on foreign soil for the first time in Boulogne. I imagined the wartime hustle and bustle of thousands of soldiers and nurses passing through ports and railway stations. I imagined the wooden framed houses and gothic cathedral in Rouen. I imagined journeying through strange French towns and villages in the back of a cattle truck and sleeping in old, deserted cottages and barns. I imagined seeing buildings turned to rubble by shells, fields turned to muddy craters and trees turned to burnt skeletons. I imagined advancing through a forest in the torrential rain with burning branches crashing down around me and grenades and gun fire all around. I imagined incredible pain and being carried on a stretcher to an Aid Post, and then onto a Casualty Clearing Station carried by a horse drawn ambulance. I imagined lying in pain overnight in a strange building in a French town I've never heard of. And then I imagined everything stopping...

Following his death, Allen's 'Dorothy Bag' with his personal belongings in, would have been sent home to his family in Chesterblade from Number 3 CSS in Caudry. His Dorothy Bag has large blotches of blood soaked into the material and receiving his possessions in this bloodied bag must have been truly awful for the family.

Allen's bloodstained cloth Dorothy Bag that contained his possessions

Allen's posthumous army pay record

After researching local records it seems Allen's father, Sidney, had to travel to Exeter in 1919 on three occasions to collect pay that was due to Allen for serving in the army. On 8 March he collected £2/15s/7d, on 23 April he collected half a shilling, and on 12 December he collected £3, but only after proof of identity had been produced. You would think it might have been kinder to have saved a grieving father the indignity of this situation, and allowed this to have been done in one visit or even to have it sent to their family address. It's hard to imagine what it would have felt like to have been summoned and drip-fed your dead son's army pay in such a manner.

The final old documents to come out of the Dorothy Bag were dated 1921 and related to war medals that had been issued to Allen posthumously.

In the attic bag were two medals. The silver-coloured British War Medal was heavy and around the size of the palm of my hand and still had its orange, blue and white ribbons attached. The King's head was on one side and a cavalier on horseback was on the other. The bronze Allied Victory Medal was the same size and weight and had a winged Britannia on one side and the words '*THE GREAT WAR FOR CIVILISATION 1914-1918*' on the other. A rainbow coloured ribbon was still attached.

I tried to consider how the family would have felt receiving this in 1921, some three years after their son had been killed; a mixture of pride and renewed anguish I imagined.

A letter received with Allen's war medals

Allen's war medals

The final object that came out of the Dorothy Bag was a square and flat white cardboard box. Upon lifting its flaps, we found inside an oversized, dark-coloured bronze coin around five inches in diameter that sat heavy in the hand; the 'Dead Man's Penny' as it came to be known. On one side, Britannia held a trident beside a lion, and two dolphins swam around the edge; a symbol of Britain's sea power. A second lion at the base tore apart a German eagle. In Britannia's outstretched left hand she held an olive wreath below which a rectangular tablet bore Allen's name (which had been spelt incorrectly). The other side of the coin was blank save for the words around the edge; 'HE DIED FOR FREEDOM AND HONOUR'. A public competition had been held to determine the design of this Memorial Plaque, and one million three hundred and fifty-five thousand were issued to the next of kin of all service personnel killed in the war.

Allen's 'Dead Man's Penny'

The final part of my French journey tracing Allen's time in France was to follow his trail from the Mormal Forest where he had fallen, to the CCS in Caudry where he died, and finally to the cemetery on the edge of the town where he had been buried. With acorns from the forest in my pocket, I walked back the two or three miles through the forest to my car at the forest edge where Allen's attack had begun and drove the fifteen miles to Caudry.

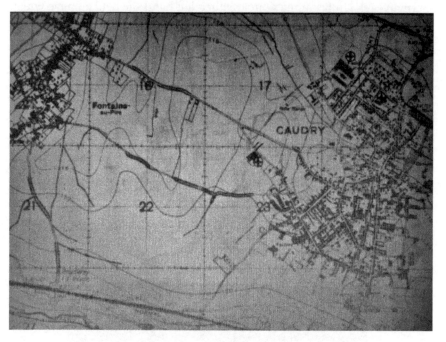

Location of the three CCS in Caudry in 1918 demarked by red crosses (reproduced by kind permission of The National Library of Scotland)

Three CCS had been based in Caudry and these were marked by red crosses on an old wartime map. By cross referencing this with the old photo of the Number 3 CCS building, and from the description given by the visiting head nurse in her diary, I deciphered Allen's CCS was the most westerly of the three on the map. This would have been along what was now Rue Henri

Barbusse. Upon arrival in Caudry, I drove along the road with a photo of the building to see if it still stood. The building no longer existed and the site where it stood was somewhat ironically a rubble site much like many buildings had been a hundred years ago. A large billboard announced the site was to be developed soon. I got out the car and paused for a moment at the place where a nineteen-year-old farm kid from rural Somerset had come to die. In the Matron-in-Chief's diary, she wrote '*the Staff were accommodated in a fine Chateau quite close*', so after some online investigation and studying maps I worked out the chateau would have been just up the road off Rue de Cambrai. As I approached the location a sign on a side street read 'Rue du Chateau' at the end of which was 'Clos du Chateau'. There was no chateau anymore, only the familiar newly built red brick houses. I tried to imagine the lives of the nurses going back and forth between their accommodation at the chateau with its windows blown out and the wounded and dying at the makeshift hospital down the road. I wondered which of them had treated and cared for Allen in his last hours alive and packed away all his letters and belongings into the bloodstained Dorothy Bag to send back to his family in Somerset.

The site of Number 3 CCS in 2018 where Allen died on 5 November 1918

I passed through the 'centre ville' and parked outside the 'Hôtel de Ville' which stood opposite a fountain and a war memorial for the local fallen. A large red brick church could be seen through a street to the side. Across the square, I noticed a tourist visitor centre so went inside and looked through its display of leaflets. There were several sites to visit in the region in relation to La Grand Guerre. At the help desk I used more of my incompetent French language skills to ask if there was anything in Caudry in relation to the war that would be worth a visit and the lady stared fairly blankly at me and simply said, 'Non'. I cut my losses and decided it was time now to undertake the very last part of the journey to the cemetery where Allen was buried. The trip had slowly been building up to this moment and now it had arrived, I didn't want to do it because it would make the story real. I felt like I had been subconsciously putting it off as the day had progressed. The afternoon was getting late and the day was starting to lose its light, so it was now or never.

After a short drive to the eastern edge of town, the familiar green sign of a War Graves Commission site came into view and I turned up a quiet street with residential houses on one side and, after a short row of houses, Allen's cemetery appeared on the other. Some young motorcyclists were undergoing training drills from an instructor on the far side of the car park, as I made my way to the cemetery entrance. The air had turned cold as the day faded. From the neatly trimmed grass at the entrance to the cemetery, grand Portland stone steps lead up to a grass plateau, in the centre of which sat the familiar Portland stone cross with brass sword set against it. To either side and around to the left, lay around seven hundred Allied graves, fifty of which remained unnamed and unidentified. The majority were British soldiers but alongside them were graves from the Chinese Labour Corps, New Zealand, Australia, South Africa, India and Canada.

Caudry British Cemetery

The familiar large slab of Portland stone with the words 'THEIR NAME LIVETH FOR EVERMORE' seen in every British cemetery, sat near the back with a row of Chinese Labour Corps headstones nearby. Most of the Chinese deaths appeared to have been in April 1919 so they had probably died from mine clearing in the area after the war. Chinese lettering spelt out their names and where they had come from in China. Various slogans honoured their sacrifice, such as '*A NOBLE DUTY BRAVELY DONE*' and '*THOUGH DEAD HE STILL LIVETH*'. Behind the row of Chinese headstones, row upon row of German gravestones in their adjacent cemetery could be seen. Their headstones were in marked contrast to the British style. They were smaller and cut with rough edges in the shape of the German cross. Most crosses had two soldiers' names etched onto each cross and often another two names on the other side, so four bodies per one headstone. It felt odd, yet strangely appropriate, seeing enemy graves in the same graveyard next to each other when you considered the person lying next to them may well have been responsible for their death. It felt inherently sad to see so many young men, many just teenagers, lying dead next to each other, but maybe there is some hope for humanity in the fact that opposing nations can forgive each other enough to lie together in death.

British gravestones in the Caudry war cemetery

Chinese Labour Corps gravestones in the British Cemetery in Caudry, with a German cemetery
directly behind

Allen's grave in Caudry British Cemetery

After putting it off until the last moment, I walked over to the far right hand side of the British cemetery to the last row where I knew Allen's grave was located. As I walked down the row, his fellow dead were teenagers and in their early twenties, and halfway along his headstone came into view. I stood there gawking at it for a while; '*42915 PRIVATE, A. J. GREEN, DORSETSHIRE REGIMENT, 5TH NOVEMBER 1918*'. Above the words, the castle regimental emblem of the Dorsets is inscribed onto the stone. This moment had been a long time coming and it was hard to take in. That I'm the first person from his family to visit his grave since his death a hundred years ago filled me with sadness for the young man. He would be forever nineteen, yet older than us all. A strange conundrum.

Inscription on the shelter wall in Caudry British Cemetery

As I looked up and surveyed the hundreds of other graves and the French town beyond, my overriding feeling was 'Allen, you don't belong here, you should be buried in the churchyard at home in Chesterblade with your brother, Jim, and your parents. What are you doing here?' He seemed completely out of place. It seemed wrong. It was the equivalent of picking a random foreign country you have never been to, then picking a random town in that country, and then deciding that was where you are going to die and be buried in isolation from any of your family. I began thinking if there could be a way of getting him brought back to England to be buried next to his brother. I wondered if this had ever been requested by relatives back in England. It felt like it would be good to get him away from the madness that took place here and get him back to the Somerset countryside. Passing through Caudry earlier that day, it had seemed like a perfectly pleasant sort of town, but it felt strange a family member was buried there; the place had no meaning to our family other than the random set of events that led to his death in the town.

I had brought with me from England a small wooden cross with a poppy attached that had the words 'IN REMEMBRANCE' written underneath. In black pen I wrote on the cross 'ALLEN, REST IN PEACE, LOVE FROM THE GREEN FAMILY, CHESTERBLADE'. I found myself talking to him for a while and I told him about my journey across France and all the discoveries I had uncovered about his life over the last year. The light had now drained quickly from the day and it felt like time to go. I made my way over to a small three-sided building behind the cross. In there, as in all British war cemeteries I had been to, sat a metal safe inset into the wall with the words 'CEMETERY REGISTER' embossed onto it. Inside the safe was a register of all the men buried in the British cemetery and their location by plot and row, and a visitor book. I took out the visitor book and looked through the other entries. The last visitor had been on 3rd January, just over a month ago, from New Zealand. Before that visitors had come from Sedgley in England, New Zealand again, Northumberland, Ireland, Essex, New Zealand again, Canada, Wigan, Shropshire and so on. In May last year I noticed a local family from Glastonbury had visited a relative, a twenty-three-year-old Captain H.W. Goodson from Allen's Dorsetshire Regiment who had died on 11 October 1918. I turned back to the latest page and left a long overdue message for Allen and placed the two registers back in the safe.

On the back wall of the shelter was an inscription in both English and French found in every British war cemetery in France. It read 'THE LAND ON WHICH THIS CEMETERY STANDS IS THE FREE GIFT OF THE FRENCH PEOPLE FOR THE PERPETUAL RESTING PLACE OF THOSE OF THE ALLIED ARMIES WHO FELL IN THE WAR OF 1914-18 AND ARE HONOURED HERE'. It was a touching sentiment. The inscription did make me wonder about the relationship the French have with the German graves on their soil having been invaded by them twice during two world wars.

A French military cemetery and war memorial in Caudry

I decided to go back to Allen's graveside and bade him a final farewell for now but resolved to visit more often in the coming years now that I had made this connection with him. On my way back to the car, I passed through the French communal cemetery next door. In the centre, I chanced upon a French military memorial and collection of gravestones, the first I had seen on this trip. On average, nine hundred French people died every day over the four years of the war. French graves are marked by a white stone cross about knee height with a white, blue and red coloured plaque attached with the soldier's name on.

As I drove back to my accommodation, I thought about the extraordinary day I had experienced and passed yet another war cemetery just outside Le Cateau, so I stopped to pay my respects feeling in a bit of a daze.

The German part of the international war cemetery near Le Cateau

I stopped to read the information board at the entrance to the cemetery:

'In the number and variety of different graves it contains, the Cateau-Cambresis international military cemetery is witness to the severity of the war in this sector … The area around Le Cateau was taken by German troops on August 26th 1914 and was liberated … on October 10th 1918, although it needed another week to mop up the last pockets of German resistance … Le Cateau was an important railhead for the Germans, and above all the location for a large number of military hospitals. Numerous wounded men were brought here from other sectors along the front line. Within the cemetery precinct lie the remains of around 5000 Germans … Alongside them are 34 graves of Russian prisoners who died in captivity and over 700 British graves. The contrast between the two main parts of this international cemetery is striking: whilst the natural vegetation is mastered and under control on the British side, it still holds sway in the German part.'

On the information board, a translation is given in both French and German. I presumed a British person had written this rather sniffy text and wondered what any Germans reading it would feel about it. That led me to wonder if many Germans come and visit their war dead in a country they invaded with such notoriety. When I entered the cemetery and walked between the different international grave sections, I had to admit the person who wrote the words on the information board had a point. The British part, as always, was respectfully well-kept in honour of those who lay there in their graves and in recognition of their sacrifice. The German part did look uncared for and unloved. There were no neatly kept shrub beds, the grass was untidy and muddy in places, ivy and brambles grew around the Russian prisoner of war graves, and a broken off headstone had been left unceremoniously to be subsumed by the grass growing around it. In contrast to the uniformity of the Commonwealth graves where rank bore no importance, higher ranked German soldiers had larger, grander looking headstones in a more opulent style than the standard rough cut cross that the lower ranks were commemorated with. That said, I felt the tone of the British information board wasn't entirely necessary.

Back at my accommodation, I looked out of the window at the Mormal Forest and thought about all that had taken place there. It had been an amazing journey over the last few days and one I had been meaning to do for years, so I felt glad I had finally undertaken it and someone from the family had been to visit Allen. I hoped my children would one day read this book and follow Allen's path across France to learn about his experiences during the war. I hoped they would honour and remember those who sacrificed their lives for us all and would visit his grave. I hoped they would learn the lessons of war and strive to prevent it ever happening again in their lifetime or those of their own children. There would always be disagreements and issues to resolve with our European neighbours, but surely we would never again want to return to the insanity and destruction seen in the two world wars on European soils. There must always remain a resolve to settle things with communication and compromise for the greater peace.

IT LEAVES ME THE SAME

For the first time in one hundred years
I visit your grave.
But I hope you are well
As it leaves me the same.

I am your kin, your blood, your descendant;
Still scratching the same piece of dirt
From here to there,
Still fingering the same seed into it,
Still watching the same shoots push
Up through the surface.

I still rub alongside the same hairy beasts,
Still occupy a place
Out in the wind, rain and pestilence.

Only a few do so now.

Much is as it was and much has changed.

You will remain forever nineteen.
A boy, yet older than us all.

APPENDIX

1. ALLEN'S JOURNEY

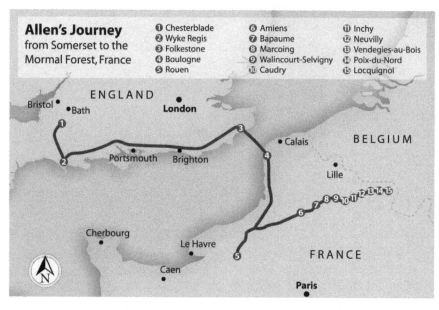

Allen's journey from Somerset to the Mormal Forest in France

2. THE WAR POETS

The war poet Wilfred Owen had fought in the same battle and died on the same day as Allen, and was buried in Ors, just south of Caudry where Allen was buried. Alongside Siegfried Sassoon, who Owen befriended towards the end of the war, Owen was one of the most prominent war poets I studied when at school. I didn't know then of the connection he would come to have with my family or that I would one day visit his grave on my journey through France to visit my great uncle's grave. Sassoon was also buried locally in the nearby village of Mells in Somerset.

Initially, Owen's work lay in relative obscurity until the 1960s when he became championed by renowned poets of the day and was included in a number of published collections of poems. From then on, he started to enjoy recognition as not only a serious poet in his own right, but also as a unique commentator on the Great War.

Two of Owen's poems stick with me now and seem most resonant with Allen's experiences and untimely death. The first speaks of his departure from the camp by train, never to return to his village lanes he knows so well.

THE SEND-OFF

Down the close darkening lanes they sang their way
To the siding-shed,
And lined the train with faces grimly gay.

Their breasts were stuck all white with wreath and spray
As men's are, dead.

Dull porters watched them, and a casual tramp
Stood staring hard,
Sorry to miss them from the upland camp.

Then, unmoved, signals nodded, and a lamp
Winked to the guard.

So secretly, like wrongs hushed-up, they went.
They were not ours:
We never heard to which front these were sent.

Nor there if they yet mock what women meant
Who gave them flowers.

Shall they return to greetings of great bells
In wild train-loads?
A few, a few, too few for drums and yells,

May creep back, silent, to village wells,
Up half-known roads.

Wilfred Owen

The second poem is a requiem for a young life lost.

ANTHEM FOR DOOMED YOUTH

What passing-bells for these who die as cattle?
- Only the monstrous anger of the guns.
Only the stuttering rifles' rapid rattle
Can patter out their hasty orisons.

No mockeries now for them; no prayers nor bells;
Nor any voice of mourning save the choirs, -
The shrill, demented choirs of wailing shells;
And bugles calling for them from sad shires.

What candles may be held to speed them all?
Not in the hands of boys, but in their eyes
Shall shine the holy glimmers of goodbyes.
The pallor of girls' brows shall be their pall;
Their flowers the tenderness of patient minds,
And each slow dusk a drawing-down of blinds.

During my journey across France following Allen's path, I also visited Owen's grave in Ors just south of where Allen was buried. To the south west of the Mormal Forest, Ors was a small village adjacent to woodland called Bois-l'Évêque. As I drove towards Ors I passed through the Bois-l'Évêque woodland, crossed a railway line and parked on a grass verge at the edge of the village. A sign marked the beginning of a walking trail that had been established in honour of Owen. The trail followed the path of his last battle that had led to his death. As at Vendegies-au-Bois, the small lanes, grass fields, hedges and trees were reminiscent of Somerset. It was picturesque and hard to believe war once raged through there. As I got ready to set off on the three mile trail, a light brown and white dog appeared by my side, and as I began the walk he started to accompany me along my way. After crossing grass fields for half a mile, I came across a walled British war cemetery in a field. My canine friend had strangely stayed with me. I couldn't see anyone else around but the dog seemed happy jogging along at my side. Despite being located in a field in the middle of nowhere, the same high standard of care was given to those buried here. The usual Portland stone cross and bronze sword looked down like a parent over the neatly kept graves of the one hundred and two men who died here. An information board read:

From August 1918 onwards, the Allies launched a major offensive forcing the German Army to withdraw from territory it had been occupying ever since

1914. The crossing of the Sambre-Oise canal was planned to take place on the 4th November. In the face of fire from the German troops dug in at a farm on the opposite bank, Wilfred Owen and his men were mown down while trying to cross the canal on a pontoon bridge. The soldiers who were killed were interred in the Ors British Cemetery and in the military section of the village cemetery.

The Canal de la Sambre where Wilfred Owen died crossing on 4 November 1918
and my canine companion

Owen was buried in the village cemetery rather than this one in the field. I wrote a message in the visitor book kept in the metal safe in the wall and continued on Owen's trail. After crossing more grass fields, I came to the large canal where Owen, aged twenty-five, and his men were mown down by enemy fire during the same attack and on the same day Allen was fatally wounded a little further north in the Mormal Forest. Looking across the canal at the farm where the Germans were dug in and fired from as Owen and his men crossed, I tried to imagine what it would have been like. With no cover, Owen and his men had been sent on a death mission with not much chance of succeeding or survival. Second-Lieutenant James Kirk was one of those killed during this mission, and he was posthumously awarded the Victoria Cross. The citation for him gave a flavour of what had happened. It read:

For most conspicuous bravery and devotion to duty North of Ors on 4th Nov., 1918, whilst attempting to bridge the Oise Canal. To cover the bridging of the canal he took a Lewis gun, and, under intense machine-gun fire, paddled across the canal on a raft, and at a range of ten yards expended all his ammunition. Further ammunition was paddled across to him and he continuously maintained a covering fire for the bridging party from a most exposed position till killed at his gun. The supreme contempt of danger and magnificent self-sacrifice displayed by this gallant officer prevented many casualties and enabled two platoons to cross the bridge before it was destroyed.

The trail continued along the gently flowing waters of the wide canal and my new four-legged friend and I followed it with not another soul in sight. The demeanour of the dog was so tranquil and in keeping with the personality that Owen was said to have had, that a fanciful feeling came over me that this creature who had acted as a guide and companion to me along the trail was somehow Owen's animal spirit. A spirit who now lived here in perpetuity to accompany those who visited the place where Owen would forever rest. As we approached a bridge across the canal up ahead, the dog and I made our way through the village, passing the church and arrived at the communal village cemetery. Towards the back of the cemetery, a British war section appeared.

The British section of Ors village cemetery where Wilfred Owen is buried

Owen's grave was one of fifty-nine that lay there. His parents received the news of his death on Armistice Day, as Allen's parents did. Owen's grave occupied a place in the back row of headstones by the hedgerow over which the picturesque village and its church could be seen amongst the trees. Someone had placed a small wooden cross and poppy at the base of his headstone. An inscription on his gravestone at the insistence of his mother read 'SHALL LIFE RENEW THESE BODIES? OF A TRUTH ALL DEATH WILL HE ANNUL'. After staying a while, I left the cemetery and said farewell to my dog-spirit friend as I reached my car. It had been a surreal experience sharing the trail with him, but I wouldn't have wanted it any other way.

In the middle of the Bois-l'Évêque woodland next to Ors, I headed towards another memorial to Owen: a forester's smokehouse where he used to stay at times during the war. Turner prize-winning artist Simon Patterson renovated and converted the old building in 2011 as an art installation and memorial to Owen, with the cellar where he used to stay restored back to its original state. An exhibition of his writing and life are on the walls upstairs. Curved walls outside have inscribed on them excerpts from his last letter home to his mother before he died and follow a sloping ramp into the white painted building. Owen had stayed here the night before he died.

The forester's smokehouse near Ors now converted into a memorial to Wilfred Owen

His last letter home to his mother read:

Dearest Mother,

I will call the place from which I'm now writing 'The Smoky Cellar of the Forester's House'. I write on the first sheet of the writing pad which came in the parcel yesterday. Luckily the parcel was small, as it reached me just before we moved off to the line. Thus only the paraffin was unwelcome in my pack. My servant & I ate the chocolate in the cold middle of last night, crouched under a draughty Tamboo, roofed with planks. I husband the Malted Milk for tonight and tomorrow night. The handkerchief and socks are most opportune, as the ground is marshy, and I have a slight cold!

So thick is the smoke in this cellar that I can hardly see by a candle 12 inches away, and so thick are the inmates that I can hardly write for pokes, nudges, and jolts. On my left, the Coy. commander snores on a bench, other officers repose on wire beds behind me. At my right hand, Kellett, a delightful servant of A Coy. in the Old days radiates joy & contentment from pink cheeks and baby eyes. He laughs with a signaller, to whose left ear is glued the receiver; but whose eyes rolling with gaiety show that he is listening with his right ear to a merry corporal, who appears at this distance away (some three feet) nothing [but] a gleam of white teeth & a wheeze of jokes.

Splashing my hand, an old soldier with a walrus moustache peels & drops potatoes in the pot. By him, Keyes, my cook, chops wood; another feeds the smoke with the damp wood.

It is a great life. I am more oblivious than alas! yourself, dear Mother, of the ghastly glimmering of the guns outside & the hollow crashing of the shells.

There is no danger down here - or if any, it will be well over before you read these lines.

I hope you are as warm as I am, as serene in your room as I am here; and that you think of me never in bed as resignedly as I think of you always in bed. Of this I am certain you could not be visited by a band of friends half so fine as surround me here.

Ever Wilfred X

After joining the Manchester regiment in June 1916 as a second-Lieutenant, Owen originally disliked what he perceived as his fellow troops' loutish behaviour. As the war progressed, his affection grew for his comrades as their shared experiences brought them together. Owen was diagnosed as suffering from shell shock in 1917 after being blown up by a mortar bomb and lying unconscious for several days on an embankment among the remains of a fellow officer. Following this he was sent for treatment to Craiglockhart War Hospital near Edinburgh where he would meet the already celebrated war poet Siegfried Sassoon. This proved to be a significant relationship and under Sassoon's mentorship Owen's poetry developed and progressed immensely.

Sassoon was at Craiglockhart after making a lone protest in 1917 at the continuation of the war via publication in the national press of his 'Soldier's Declaration'. A sympathetic MP also read out the declaration in Parliament. In it he said *'I am making this statement as an act of wilful defiance of military authority ... I believe that the war upon which I entered as a war of defence and liberation has now become a war of aggression and conquest'*. Sassoon believed the war was now being prolonged longer than necessary, and the continued slaughter of his fellow troops was unjustified. Having been decorated for bravery while serving on the Western Front, Sassoon's until then exemplary service record meant that rather than being held for treason, he was seen as psychiatrically unstable due to shell shock, and he was sent to Craiglockhart for treatment. His friend and fellow war poet, Robert Graves, was instrumental in rigging the committee meeting where Sassoon's fate was decided so his friend was not held for treason. Graves' autobiographical 'Goodbye To All That' covers this and his own wartime experiences and stands as one of the few detailed first person pieces of prose on the reality of the trenches.

Pat Barker's book *Regeneration* provides a fictional account of Sassoon's time at Craiglockhart and the moral dilemma he faced while there; should he assume a position of pacifism and oppose the war in safety, should he wait out the war in safety under a diagnosis of shell shock, or should he return to France to fight not in support of the war but in support of his fellow troops to help them survive? Sassoon had become known for his paradoxical near suicidal acts of bravery in France in order to lead and protect his men whom he admired, whilst fostering a growing depression and anger at the continuing misery and terror they had to endure. He had been awarded the Military Cross with the citation reading *'For conspicuous gallantry during a raid on the enemy's trenches. He remained for 1½ hours under rifle and bomb fire collecting and bringing in our wounded. Owing to his courage and determination all the killed and wounded were brought in.'*

In the end, Sassoon chose to declare himself sane, and left Craiglockhart in July 1918 and returned to France to help his men but was almost immediately wounded in the head by friendly fire after being mistaken for a German during an attack. He subsequently returned to England where he remained until the end of the war. Sassoon would go on to live to the age of eighty and is buried in Mells only a few miles from Allen's home in Somerset.

Owen could have remained in England after being admitted to Craiglockhart, but chose also to return to France, replicating Sassoon. He saw it as his duty to continue to write vivid accounts through his poetry of the realities of the war, especially once he knew Sassoon had returned permanently to England. After the war, Sassoon was instrumental in getting Owen's poems a wider audience, as Owen had only ever had five poems published before his death. Another war poet, Edmund Blunden, published a full edition of Owen's poems in 1931 which brought more prominence to Owen's work. It wasn't until the 1960s, however, that Owen would receive the recognition for his poetry that we acknowledge today. On 11 November 1985, sixteen war poets, including all those mentioned above, were acknowledged with the unveiling of a plaque in Westminster Abbey in Poet's Corner. The inscription chosen was a quote of Owen's. It read, *'My subject is War, and the pity of War. The Poetry is in the pity.'*

It seems apt to end this part of the book with another poem. Owen's poem 'Strange Meeting' was set in the underworld where a soldier has gone to escape the horrors of the war above, only to find himself faced with an enemy soldier he had killed the day before.

STRANGE MEETING

It seemed that out of battle I escaped
Down some profound dull tunnel, long since scooped
Through granites which titanic wars had groined.

Yet also there encumbered sleepers groaned,
Too fast in thought or death to be bestirred.
Then, as I probed them, one sprang up, and stared
With piteous recognition in fixed eyes,
Lifting distressful hands, as if to bless.
And by his smile, I knew that sullen hall,—
By his dead smile I knew we stood in Hell.

With a thousand fears that vision's face was grained;
Yet no blood reached there from the upper ground,
And no guns thumped, or down the flues made moan.
'Strange friend,' I said, 'here is no cause to mourn.'
'None,' said that other, 'save the undone years,
The hopelessness. Whatever hope is yours,
Was my life also; I went hunting wild
After the wildest beauty in the world,
Which lies not calm in eyes, or braided hair,
But mocks the steady running of the hour,

And if it grieves, grieves richlier than here.
For by my glee might many men have laughed,
And of my weeping something had been left,
Which must die now. I mean the truth untold,
The pity of war, the pity war distilled.
Now men will go content with what we spoiled.
Or, discontent, boil bloody, and be spilled.
They will be swift with swiftness of the tigress.
None will break ranks, though nations trek from progress.
Courage was mine, and I had mystery;
Wisdom was mine, and I had mastery:
To miss the march of this retreating world
Into vain citadels that are not walled.
Then, when much blood had clogged their chariot-wheels,
I would go up and wash them from sweet wells,
Even with truths that lie too deep for taint.
I would have poured my spirit without stint
But not through wounds; not on the cess of war.
Foreheads of men have bled where no wounds were.

'I am the enemy you killed, my friend.
I knew you in this dark: for so you frowned
Yesterday through me as you jabbed and killed.
I parried; but my hands were loath and cold.
Let us sleep now...'

3. Farming after the Great War

The war had taken men and horses from farms, and replaced them with women and tractors. The supply of enough food had come under intense pressure during the war due to German attacks on ships bringing in food imports and due to the lack of manpower and horsepower to produce the food on farms. New innovations and machinery took time to develop and workers needed time to learn how to use them, but by the end of the war, machines were coming into their own.

The effect of this was that men returning home from the war were now no longer needed as much. Mechanisation had replaced them. More food was being produced more efficiently now, leading to an over-supply of food after the war as supply outstripped demand, and food prices dropped. In other industries too, increasing mechanisation caused unemployment rates to rise. It must have been an awful situation for many returning traumatised and injured from war to find they were now no longer wanted in the workplace. Those returning home also struggled to fit back into domestic life. In Robert Graves' memoir 'Goodbye To All That', he described how after the war there were lost souls traversing the country searching for work and living rough in the countryside feeding off hedgerows for food. Resuming family relationships after enduring the experience of war wasn't possible for many, both for those returning and for those who had stayed behind and kept the home fires burning.

But it wasn't just people that had left home and been sent to war. Half a million horses had been commandeered from farms in the UK and their futures were now uncertain once the Armistice had been announced. Horses had suffered harsh conditions at the front as they faced illness and death from poison gas, artillery fire, starvation and skin disorders. Veterinary hospitals were established to treat them and get them back to the front and in certain circumstances they were thought of as a more important loss than men. Hundreds of thousands of horses had died. At the start of the war all the armies fought with cavalry but as the war progressed and the mechanisation of war increased, the horses' role became more logistical. Horses had been more adept than vehicles traversing rough ground and mud, and had become integral to the movement of supplies, munitions, large wheeled guns and battlefield ambulances.

There were countless stories recounting the bonds that formed between man and horse during the war, and I can imagine how important these relationships would have been to both parties when faced with such abhorrent circumstances. Such intimate relationships would have provided a much needed solace and some would have travelled together with their horse when called up to war. I discovered a story of a Pembrokeshire farmer's grandfather who was taken prisoner in 1916 by the Germans. He thought his cavalry horse, Grey Lady, had been killed during the battle. The grandfather had survived the war and was attending a horse show back home in 1926 when a horse whinnied at him as he walked by – it was Grey Lady! The two were reunited and he brought Grey Lady back with him after the show and the two remained together for the rest of her life.

Once the war came to an end, the only horses guaranteed a return home were officers' mounts. For the rest, age and fitness determined their fate. The British Army brought home twenty-five thousand of the youngest and healthiest and another sixty thousand were sold to farmers. Below this threshold, horses were auctioned off to farmers on the continent, and those too old and no longer fit to work were killed in abattoirs and sold for meat as food shortages hit a devastated Europe.

The contribution these amazing animals made to the war effort has been remembered in various ways. During the Armistice remembrance in 1920, the carriage of the Unknown Soldier was pulled by a team of six horses, the Old Blacks, who had served throughout the whole war. The Horse Trust managed to save some horses and retire them into stables they owned. One such of these, Roger, was rescued after he was found wandering in No Man's Land on a battlefield in France. During the war, the RSPCA had helped care for horses, and after the conflict had ended set up the Animals War Memorial Dispensary to help rescue and care for the thousands of war horses that had been left on the continent to a life of hard labour after what must have been a horrific experience for them. By 1932, six thousand animals had been treated and the clinic still runs today. The Ada Cole Stables rescued war horses from the Belgian horse markets right through into the 1930s. Since the war, several memorials have been erected to commemorate the contribution made by horses.

4. ALLEN'S MATE, CARY

In Allen's letters, he mentioned on numerous occasions a friend he calls
Cary. Herbert Cary was born the same year as Allen in 1899 and his family
were farmers at Dangerfield Farm in Buckland Dinham, a small village
twelve miles from Chesterblade where Allen lived. Herb registered with the
army on 28 April 1917 and was mobilised into the 3rd Dorsetshire Regiment
on 19 June 1918, around the same time as Allen. The two friends trained
together at the Wyke Regis camp near Weymouth and travelled to France
together on the boat from Folkestone to Boulogne, and then on through
Rouen, Amiens, Neuvilly and the final attack through the Mormal Forest
that would see Allen killed. Herb survived the war and was discharged with
farm workers' priority to the Reserves on 29 January 1919.

Today, the Cary family still farm in Buckland Dinham, and Herb Cary's
son, Robin, still lives in the village, and Robin's son, Paul, still farms today.
I recently met with Robin and Herb's daughter, Di, who lives in Stoney
Stratton, a hamlet just two miles from Chesterblade where Allen lived. They
both said their father never talked about the war, although he did write
some memoirs in 1975 in which he touched on his experiences during
the war. Herb would travel home as often as possible, and illegally kept
a motorbike nearby in Weymouth, using petrol from the farm to get him
home and back. In France he served as a Lewis gunner alongside Allen
and eventually demobbed in January 1919. He recalls having to march one

hundred miles back to the coastal port of Treport to sail home, walking around thirty miles a day. Once on home soil, his train eventually arrived at Westbury train station, five miles from home, and he walked the rest of the way from there. He recalled encountering a local farmer, Gerald Candy, at Cherry Tree Farm on this walk back and described how touched he had been by the farmer's heartfelt welcome home.

5. Arthur Allen

Arthur Allen's family resided at Manor Farm in Chesterblade for many years. He recalled in his memoirs a passage of handwriting found in an old family bible written in 1841 by Annie Allen, a distant cousin. The passage was written in 1841 and relates to life in the area during the time of the Bristol Riots in October 1831, giving a flavour of the hard life Somerset was facing at that time. It is a fascinating piece of social history. It reads:

'THE OLD MILL
Grandmother was left a widow when her eldest son was but seventeen and her youngest more than ten years younger. She was a very capable woman, and thoroughly understood the business. "Sister" (my mother's elder sister) had for a year or two been helping my grandfather in the book-keeping, and my uncle grew up suddenly under the responsibility thus early thrust upon him. For though grandmother, with the old miller's help, could manage the mill, and my aunt Elizabeth could keep the books, yet neither of them could attend the fairs and markets and take long rides over Mendip to the farmhouses to buy corn and cheese. All this fell to my uncle's share, and he early developed a talent for the tedious "deals" still in fashion in the West Country. So between them they managed to keep on and, after a few years, to prosper, till at length they bought the nice house and grounds at Shepton.

Yet at first they had hard times, for corn was very scarce and dear. The second winter after grandfather's death there was great distress. Bread rose to famine prices, over a shilling a loaf, I think, but mother did not remember the exact price, and the poor were almost starved and had to eat horrible stuff instead of bread, made from spoiled wheat. There were ricks burnt too, and bad people were about, so that they were all afraid for my uncle to make his business journeys over the country, yet he had to go. Folks began to talk, too, of the Bristol Reform riots, and how, from the top of the Mendips, they had seen fires Bristol way night after night. As a little child, mother had been "carried up Mendip to see Bristol burning". They talked too of Farmer Dairs, whom evil fate took up to Bristol to sell his cheese during the riots. Meeting the rioters in the streets, and getting excited at the noise, he waved his umbrella and cried, "Come on, Boys!" For this he was sentenced to death, and after hiding for six months on Mendip, he was caught and hanged.

At last, one evening when they were sitting in the parlour, the maid rushed in from the kitchen (which looked on to the road) crying, "Oh! Ma'am, they have come to burn the place down!" My uncle rose at once, "Put out all the lights, and take the children up to the garret. I will go and speak to them." Grandmother caught at his sleeve as he went by, "No, Mother, I must go; it is the only chance." When he reached the door into the road, the miller would have gone out with him, but he waved him back. "It is my risk," he said, "take care of the women and children." But Susan, grandmother's cousin, slipped out after him, and the door was shut. A hush fell on the crowd, as they saw the lad of eighteen facing them. "Friends", he said "What do you want?" And Mother, peeping through the shutters of the kitchen window, saw in the torchlight the men's faces like the faces of wild beasts from hunger, and their hands crooked like bird's claws. There were women, too, more dreadful than the men.

"Friends," he said again, "What do you want?" "Bread" they cried, "give us bread; we're starving" – "Why do you come to ask it at this time of night, and with torches? Which of you has my mother ever turned away hungry from her door? Believe me, it is hard times for us as well as you. We live as plainly as we can, and do not spend a penny we can help, and give away all we can spare. What profit will it be to you, if you burn down the house and mill, and turn my mother and her helpers' children on the parish? You will get but little corn either, for it is so dear to buy that I have no great stock, and you would throw Parfitt and Andrews, and the others, out of work. How would that help you? Better let us go on working, and I will sell you as cheaply as I can, for I will not grind the faces of the poor."

The crowd wavered and were almost won, when a voice cried from the back; "Will you be put off by fair words and empty promises? Come on lads and force the door." Howling like wolves, the men again pressed forward, but my uncle stood his ground. "Empty promises? Who ever knew my father break his word? See now, to show you I mean what I say, I will give to each of you who is a married man from Downside or Shepton, a written order for a stone of flour at half-price. Bring it to me, or send it by your wives to-morrow morning, and you shall have the flour."

The men stopped and my uncle took out his pocket book. Susan, stepping out from behind him, called out, "If you will go away, we will send you a barrel of beer down to the Market Place first thing to-morrow morning." The starving men raised a cheer. "Right you are, Missus, mind you don't forget." My uncle wrote the name of the man nearest him in his pocket-book with the promise of the stone of flour and handed him the leaf. The others crowded round my uncle, holding their torches so that he might see to write. "No, not him, sir, he be none of us, he comes from Croscombe." – "Yes, sir, he come from Shepton, and have five children and another coming" – and so on till the married men all had their precious slips. The bachelors were inclined to make trouble, but the married men took my uncle's part. "T'aint so bad for you, you fellows, as you have no children to starve before your eyes. You can't look for the young master to give to you, when he have five mouths of his own to feed." So they all went away, and the next year the tide began to turn.'

Arthur Allen's family had been farming in and around Chesterblade since arriving from Devon in the 1500s, and as a young man Arthur boarded a ship to Australia in 1893 to find his fortune in the gold fields, running horse and cart transport teams and digging water wells. He returned home to Chesterblade after a few years of antipodean adventure to fulfil his dream of running the family farm after his father's retirement, and did so from 1905 until his own retirement in 1938. Over that time he forged a great interest and reputation as a dairy farmer and cattle breeder. My family now farm the land that was once farmed by the Allen family at Manor Farm in Chesterblade.

He also goes on to comment on its character in the 1940s:

'*Although Chesterblade is six hundred feet above sea level it is more or less secluded and sheltered, being situated at the foot of a hill on the north side, with Smalldown on the east and Maesdown on the west, leaving the south open to a wonderful view of beautiful country extending to what is known as the Dorset Heights away in the distance.*

Chesterblade is real country, approached by narrow lanes from three directions … Scores of holiday makers who visit Chesterblade in the summer months climb to the summit of Smalldown from which they are able to obtain a glorious, uninterrupted view of the surrounding country.

Apart from all its other advantages, this hamlet is, as it were, tucked away on its own, free from the rush and roar of modern vehicle traffic which flood the majority of the roads of our countryside today and, above all, it remains unspoilt by modern red-brick and tiled buildings which seem to be the fashion in all the towns and villages now-a-days.'

6. THE GREEN FAMILY AFTER THE GREAT WAR

With the eldest son, Allen, no longer on the farm, his younger brother, Jim, my grandfather, had to step up and fill his shoes to help the family run the farm. When his older brother died in 1918, Jim was eleven years old. When he was thirteen years old in 1920, he left school and came home to help run the farm full time. What a different life he would have had if his older brother had survived.

Wilfred Hares fought with the Somerset Light Infantry during the war in Mesopotamia and had responsibility for dealing with the horses. After the war, Wilfred came and worked on our farm in Chesterblade and I have many memories of working as a child alongside Wilfred and my grandfather. Wilfred lived at Banks House, a cottage opposite the main farmyard, and he and my grandfather were both keen gardeners and kept huge gardens full of vegetables and fruit. In Wilfred's garden there was an old Second World War air-raid shelter turned shed, and it was a tool repair emporium. Back then, anything that was required was made on the farm if possible, and everything that broke was mended.

Wilfred's old tin-roofed shed had an old self-made wooden door with peeling green paint, and inside the walls were lined with homemade wooden shelves bowed heavy with old paint tins filled with old rusty nails, screws, hinges and miscellaneous fittings to be used on forthcoming repair projects. On hooks hung a huge selection of old fashioned hand drills, hammers, screwdrivers, chisels and scythes. A wobbly wooden workbench held a metal vice in which dozens of pitch fork handles and the like would be renewed and repaired. I used to love going into the shed to help out with repairs.

Out on the farm, I have distinct memories of pitchforking around grass silage on top of the silage pits with Wilfred and my grandfather as the trailers brought in the grass from the fields and tipped out their loads. My father pushed the grass up onto the pits with a buck rake on the back of an old Universal tractor. A favourite saying of Wilfred's was 'one boy is a whole boy, two boys are half a boy, and three boys are no good at all'. This was often recounted to me if there were any other farm worker kids around on the farm 'helping' when I was there. Another seasonal task that sticks in the memory is the annual log chopping in the autumn to fill up the log stores with firewood for the winter. A saw-bench with a spinning jagged edged circular blade would be attached on the back of a tractor and this would whizz noisily around at great speed. Dad would push lengths of fallen branches onto the spinning blade and cut them into logs small enough to be used in the open fires at home. I would then stack the cut logs with my grandfather and Wilfred into the logs stores, an act of stacking precision that I would be chastised for if not done correctly.

Wilfred eventually retired aged seventy-eight in 1979 and remained living alone in the farm cottage until 1989, when he became too incapacitated to live alone and moved into a retirement home. It was common then for a farm worker to have a job and a house for life in recognition of the contribution made to the farm. I would often go and visit Wilfred with my grandfather when farm jobs had been caught up with, and sit with them having a cup of tea and chewing the fat in Wilfred's old kitchen next to the Rayburn stove. We'd often bring with us a small job for Wilfred to do, like mending a pitchfork handle. The cottage had faded old-fashioned wallpaper and the musk of an elderly person's home. Thick curtains were drawn across doorways to keep the heat in. Wilfred eventually died in 1993 aged ninety-two.

My grandfather, Jim, would go on to become an innovative and pioneering farmer who became a well-known country character in the farming community. After the war, he was one of the first to start using a milking machine rather than milking by hand and built up a sizable milking herd. He rented an extra farm and bought more land and would marry Annie Sealey, a farmer's daughter from near Evercreech, in 1932. Sidney, Jim's father, died in 1947 aged seventy-nine.

Jim and Annie had four children. In memory of Jim's older brother, the second born in 1936 was named Allen, and this was my father. When my father left school, he farmed together with my grandfather at Banks Farm in Chesterblade and married my mother, Pamela Lydford, a local farmer's daughter from Stoke St. Michael, in 1964. They continued farming at Banks Farm with my grandparents and had three children. I was born in 1973, a few years after my two older sisters, and I was given the middle name Allen.

I lived in another house in the village of Chesterblade with my two older sisters and parents until I was around four years old. My grandmother became ill and it was decided our family would move in permanently with my grandparents to help look after my grandmother as the main farmhouse at Banks Farm was large enough to accommodate everyone. Between the age of five and eleven, I would spend a lot of time with my grandfather helping out on the farm. At this time I knew nothing of how he had lost his older brother back when he was around the same age as I was then. I never once heard him speak of his sibling, but I have since heard my father say how upset my grandfather had been by his death. Naming his first son Allen would have been a constant reminder to him of his lost brother.

It made for an interesting upbringing. The household consisted of my grandparents, my parents, my two older sisters, me and a couple of collie dogs. I can only just remember my grandmother, as she died in 1977 soon after we had moved in with them. My memory of her consists of an image of her in a light blue dressing gown sitting in an armchair in the kitchen. My grandfather was what you would have described as a 'character': patriarchal, full of anecdotes and tales, well respected, bloody minded, hardworking, stubborn and liable to swear like a trooper at times. My grandfather taught me a lot. I picked up more life lessons and swear words from him than from school, and I would love to be able to speak to him now to ask him about his brother and life in general.

Towards the end of his life, my grandfather became ill with pneumonia and had to go into hospital. On his death-bed on Christmas Eve in 1992 aged eighty-four, he asked for Allen. At the time we thought he was asking for his son, my father, to be present, but I wonder if he was also asking for his older brother whom he had lost all those years before. I hope that somehow the brothers have been reunited in the next world, wherever that may be. At the time of Allen's death, Jim was told that the only personal belongings that came back from France were a pair of nail scissors. He wasn't told about the personal effects bag, or the letters, post cards, and other possessions contained within it, and he never did know about the existence of these things for the rest of his life. Their sister, Elsie, had taken Allen's possessions with her when she married in 1939.

At this time Elsie was living in Cypress House in Chesterblade with her parents, Sidney and Mabel, having come back the year before from Beacon Farm where she was working on the rented farm there with my grandfather. When they all returned to Chesterblade in 1938, Sidney and Mabel moved out of Banks Farmhouse and into Cypress House, so Jim, Annie and their three children at the time (including my father) could move in. Elsie married Leonard Turner, a farmer from Alham just over the hill towards Batcombe. They were married in St. Mary's Chapel in Chesterblade and then moved to Easton Hill Farm in Pylle about six miles away. Allen's belongings and letters remained in the attic of the farmhouse for seventy-two years before they were discovered by Elsie's granddaughter, Helen, in 2011. When Mabel became ill towards the end of her life, she moved in with her daughter at Easton Hill Farm and would die here in 1947 aged seventy-five. By this time, Sidney and Mabel had previously moved into Church View house in Chesterblade. My father can recall visiting his grandfather, Sidney, after Mabel had died and remembers the grieving widower breaking down in tears as he looked at all the jams his recently departed wife had made a short while before.

I have a beautiful rectangular walnut box that once belonged to my grandfather. It is a foot wide and two feet long and has elaborate patterns embedded across it. Once unlocked, secret compartments are revealed inside behind sliding shutters and hinged doors. There are old documents from across his lifetime; his marriage and birth certificates, funeral service cards for various friends and family including his wife, ration books and identity papers from the Second World War, and a book on architecture awarded to his wife when she was a pupil in 1919 at Sunny Hill Girls School in Bruton, the same school my two daughters would later attend. There is also a rabbit's foot on a keyring, which was thought to bring good fortune, and a pair of one penny coins, one dated 1909 and one dated 1914. I wonder if the rabbit from which he made this came from one of his rabbiting sessions with his older brother from around the time he acquired these two coins?

Today, I am still running the farm at Banks Farm in Chesterblade. Before me, my father, Allen, his father, Jim, his older brother, Allen, their father Sidney, and two further generations all farmed the same land. Since the late 1700s, these six generations have toiled on this same patch of dirt and witnessed many changes, and yet much remains the same. I have planted in pots the acorns I brought home from the Mormal Forest where Allen had been fatally wounded and these will become part of a Memorial Woodland I am going to plant on the farm in Allen's memory.

The old oak tree on the farm

My favourite tree on the farm is an old oak that stands on the slope of a valley known as Westwell Bottom. It's believed to be around two hundred and seventy-five years old, so it has stood here for around the same length of time as my family. It is a family tree. The slope it grows out from is steep so the old girl has arched her spine backwards as if to retain balance and the twisted network of branches act like arms to steady herself. Her bark is old and gnarly. She is the matriarch and stateswoman of the valley. This old girl has seen the sun rise and set a great many times. Much has changed, and many different people have passed around her, and this quiet valley will outlive us all. I find it reassuring for this to be the case. The omnipresence and power of mother earth is a wonderful thing and puts the shallow and frenetic nature of human beings in their place. The pain and suffering we inflict on fellow human beings in times of war and the scarring we scratch onto the earth's surface always heals and renews as nature grows anew from the scorched earth of the battlefield. Nature is powerful and timeless and we are temporary.

Oaks have a nine hundred year lifetime, and I wonder what this old oak leaning on the side of a valley will see over the next six hundred years.

AFTERWORD – THOUGHTS FROM A MODERN PERSPECTIVE

After six months of negotiations, a formal peace treaty, the Treaty of Versailles, was signed on 28 June 1919, exactly five years after Archduke Franz Ferdinand was shot and killed, an event which had sparked the beginning of the war. The treaty required Germany and her allies to accept responsibility 'for causing all the loss and damage' of the war and this aspect of the treaty became known as the War Guilt clause. The treaty also forced Germany to disarm, give up substantial areas of territory and pay reparations to its opponents. The total cost of this was calculated to be £6.6 billion in 1921, which would equate to £284 billion today. Some thought this too harsh, such as the British economist J.M. Keynes, whilst others thought it too lenient, such as the French Marshal Ferdinand Foch. In the end the conflicting goals created a compromise that left no-one content and Germany was left neither pacified nor weakened, and these loose ends would fester and eventually lead to the outbreak of the Second World War a few years later.

It is interesting to ponder these reparations now one hundred years later as negotiations ensue between the UK and Europe following a referendum here that voted to leave the European Union. Figures currently being talked about are payments of £50 billion that the UK would have to pay the EU as a divorce settlement before trade talks can begin. Germany and France have in the last few decades become the two dominant countries within the EU, especially when it comes to the political direction of Europe. Germany has become the economic powerhouse in Europe and is well known for its productive efficiency and manufacturing prowess. Now, a hundred years on from helping save Europe, it is the UK that has to pay.

The referendum vote to leave the EU was an extremely narrow margin and it is highly likely if another vote was taken now the result could well go the other way. Since the vote, it has become apparent that the promises the 'leave' campaigners were making to voters in the run up to the vote were not as robust as claimed, and the cost of going it alone is going to be higher both in terms of the divorce bill and the loss of favourable trading terms with our most important trading partners.

It seems to me that the biggest success of the EU since its formation was peace in our time, and yet in the lead up to the referendum, this was the topic talked about the least. The campaign rhetoric was almost solely based around the fear of immigrants entering our country and a dislike of EU bureaucracy and 'being told what to do'. Across the centuries, all populations of all countries have been made up of waves of people moving from here to there on this planet. No race is 'pure' or singular and we are all made up of a mixture of bloodlines from different places. Empires that have risen and fallen have spread their peoples around the globe, and this was no different during the time of the British Empire.

With respect to some people's objections to the bureaucratic and political aspects of the EU machine, I would argue that any organisation the size of the EU is never going to be perfect, especially when it has to accommodate so many nations and find compromise between them. But if overall it provides more positive outcomes than it does negative, then it is probably best to appreciate the benefits of this rather than bemoan

imperfections. In general, there is more that unites us than divides us. It is
not surprising that ever increasing political and economic unification has
been sought by countries in mainland Europe following two world wars on
its soils, and frequent other battles over the centuries before that too.

Farming subsidies have also come under increasing criticism. Their
introduction was initially due to the fact that we almost ran out of food in
wartime because we had become so reliant on imported food. Two world
wars brought into focus the need to be self-sufficient to a degree that put the
nation at less risk. Food is the one thing you cannot do without ultimately
and it's ironic that certain politicians and people in prominence are now
returning to a position whereby we would again be reliant on importing
food. Supporting home production on UK farms is seen as an unnecessary
luxury. The global marketplace is portrayed as a reliable solution as provider
of the nation's food.

Being part of a united European block is painted as a burden we could
do without. 'Brexiters' want to live in 'beautiful isolation' on our hallowed
island, not letting anyone in, and free to trade goods in and out with whoever
we please. Becoming isolationist in a world which is ultimately made up of
a community of countries doesn't make any sense. How can it be better to
cut ourselves off from others when the world is made up of a multitude of
interconnections? It doesn't make sense either to remove ourselves from
our most important trading partners that have formed themselves into a
financially powerful trading block. The EU is our most important export
market providing as it does three hundred million affluent consumers right
on our doorstep. The majority of our imports also travel back the other way
from the EU, and our exit from this trading block will mean less favourable
terms with our most important trading partner.

Politically, I can well understand why the countries in central mainland
Europe have sought closer union as this is far more desirable than its soils

becoming a ripped up battlefield again. It is curious why the UK finds this so abhorrent. Maybe our island mentality can't cope with uniting with our neighbouring countries across the Channel and the battles with France and others over the centuries form too big a divide to bridge. I hope we overcome these reservations at some point as surely being united, even in an imperfect way, is better than isolating ourselves from our nearest neighbours and moving towards the danger of another day in the future when once again weapons are drawn against others.

However, my book is not about this, but written to commemorate the short life and sacrifice of Allen John Green. Thank you for reading his story.

Ed Green
2018

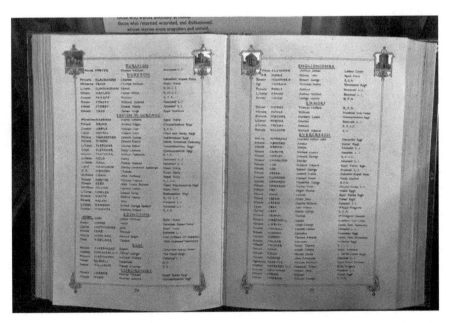

The 'Golden Book' in Wells Cathedral where all the fallen from the Great War are remembered by parish. Allen is listed on the Evercreech Parish page open above

BIBLIOGRAPHY

BOOKS

Allen, Arthur, *Passing On* (Self Published, 1946)

Barker, Pat, *Regeneration* (Penguin, 1992)

Gliddon, Jon, *Mud, Blood & Bayonet* (Choir Press, 2018)

Graves, Robert, *Goodbye To All That* (Penguin, 2000)

Guy, Revd Dr John R., *The Chapel In The Tithing* (Self Published, 1992)

Lassman, David, *Frome In The Great War* (Pen & Sword, 2016)

Silken, John ed., *First World War Poetry* (Penguin, 1985)

NOTES AND SOURCES

Keep Military Museum, Dorchester

Imperial War Museum, London

National Archives, London

Swanage Museum

Wareham Museum

WEBSITES

http://www.bbc.co.uk/schools/0/ww1/25237880

http://www.british-history.ac.uk

http://www.britishlegion.org.uk

https://www.cwgc.org

https://everydaylivesinwar.herts.ac.uk

http://www.iwm.org.uk

http://www.longlongtrail.co.uk

https://miepvonsydow.wordpress.com

https://www.nfuonline.com/about-us/history/farming-and-the-first-world-war

http://www.parsonssun.com

http://www.remembrancetrails-northernfrance.com

http://www.scarletfinders.co.uk

http://www.somersetheritage.org.uk

http://www.spiritofremembrance.com

http://www.stepshort.co.uk

https://www.theatlantic.com

http://www.yprespeacemonument.com

Allen and Ed sitting on the same chair in front of the same house

they both grew up in a hundred years apart